"I'M NOT SURE WHETHER I'M AN ACTOR WHO RACES OR A RACER WHO ACTS."

"A stretch of wide, lonely California desert in the backcountry near Indio. The sun is well up in a clear and cloudless sky. A soft wind stirs the puckerbushes, and, far off, but increasing in volume, is the faint insect buzz of a Husovarna Motocross at speed. A rider is approaching. Slamming his machine hard over the ridged sand, sliding around rocks and cactus, wheeling closer.

"The sound of the Husky is now a throbbing roar as a helmeted McQueen throttles past, tanned and shirtless, jumping a sand ditch, smiling at nothing and nobody."

* * *

Steve McQueen is a guy who loves racing. And he's raced them all—from race-tuned production models to factory prototypes and in dune buggies, modified jeeps, formula machines, brutal desert specials and on all types of competition cycles. Here now is his exciting racing story told for the first time.

STEVE McQUEEN:

STAR ON WHEELS

WILLIAM NOLAN

A BERKLEY MEDALLION BOOK
PUBLISHED BY
BERKLEY PUBLISHING CORPORATION

Published by arrangement with G. P. Putnam's Sons

SBN 425-02160-2

BERKLEY MEDALLION BOOKS published by
Berkley Publishing Corporation
200 Madison Avenue
New York, N.Y. 10016

BERKLEY MEDALLION BOOKS ® TM 757,373

Printed in the United States of America

BERKLEY MEDALLION EDITION, APRIL, 1972

To the memory of Charles and Helen Beaumont

INTRODUCTION

In his hours away from a motion picture set, Steve McQueen races. He'll have a go on anything with wheels and a hot engine. He's competed in sports cars—from race-tuned production models to factory prototypes—and in dune buggies, modified jeeps, formula machines, brutal desert specials and on many types of competition cycles. He has often declared: "I'm not sure whether I'm an actor who races or a racer who acts."

He's raced with and against such top pros as Mario Andretti, Stirling Moss, Mickey Thompson, Parnelli Jones, Pedro Rodriguez and a host of others. He's competed in the Baja 1000, the Sebring Grand Prix and the International Six-Day Trials in Germany and has run the Le Mans circuit in a 550-hp 917 Porsche.

Until now, the full racing story of McQueen has never been told. Steve has not encouraged publicity regarding his participation in racing events, since he does not wish to use the sport as a promotion device. He competes because he has a genuine respect and enthusiasm for racing—and his star status is put aside when he pulls on a crash helmet and straps himself into the cockpit of a racing machine.

The roots of this book extend back to the late 1950's, when I contributed scripts to his *Wanted* TV series. I first met him on the set and later watched him compete in his early West Coast sports car races when he drove Porsches and a fast Lotus.

Over the last dozen years, I have written several sports-racing biographies (on Phil Hill, John Fitch, Barney Oldfield, etc.), while continuing to follow Steve's career on and off the tracks. A recent magazine assignment led to our getting together for several revealing talks, and my interviews with McQueen (in which we covered his racing career in depth) form the backbone of this present biography. Thus, I have quoted him extensively throughout these pages.

The Steve McQueen story is an exciting one, and I have attempted to do it justice in this book.

WILLIAM F. NOLAN
Woodland Hills, California

1

TWELVE HOURS OF SPEED

Sebring: pines arrowing up along the horizon, the scent of orange groves, the bulk of hangars casting square black shadows under a blazing sun. Sebring: an abandoned airfield located in the center of the Florida peninsula, once the landing site for massive B-17 bombers during World War II and, beginning in 1950, annual host to the world's finest drivers. Sebring: alive again in March as a murderously tough 5.2-mile racing circuit incorporating three wide airstrips and two legs of blacktop road, site of the International Manufacturers' Championship endurance race that blasts the plains of central Florida with unmuffled automotive thunder day and night for a dozen punishing hours of speed.

In March, 1970, for the twentieth running of this classic race, 68 razor-tuned sports-racing machines had qualified for positions on the starting grid. Here were the sleekly powerful 512 factory Ferraris and the brutal Alfa Romeo T-33's from Italy, the very swift 650 Matra Spyders from France, the potent new 917 Porsches from Germany and the tough, muscular Ford GT-40's and full-race Corvettes from the United States. Top drivers were there to tame the metal beasts: Dan Gurney, co-driving a Matra, Jo Siffert and Pedro Rodriguez in Porsches, Piers Courage and Masten Gregory in Alfas, Jackie Ickx and the great Indy champ, Mario Andretti, in Ferraris. An all-star field.

In row eight, having qualified fifteenth fastest, was a white Porsche 908 Spyder, to be piloted by film actor Steve McQueen and the millionaire sportsman-driver Peter Revson. Race buffs looked on the entry with scorn; how could an underpowered 908 Porsche, entered by a screen star who was foolish enough to attempt to operate the clutch pedal with a broken left foot, ever hope to compete on a professional level against the finest and fastest European cars and drivers?

"Maybe McQueen thinks he's in another Hollywood movie," one Sebring veteran remarked. "He's got a big shock in store for him when that flag drops, because these boys sure aren't following any script!"

The original plan had called for each man to drive for an hour, then pit and turn the car over to his co-driver. But Steve had decided to take on a two-hour double shift at the wheel of the 908, "in order to sort myself out and see how my foot would hold up under full-race conditions." He wore what he jokingly called "my Frankenstein boot," which consisted of a custom-made reinforced leather boot designed to fit over his cut-down plaster cast. A strip of sandpaper was glued to the bottom in order to provide more traction on the clutch pedal.

"I smashed the first cast practicing with the 908 back in California," McQueen declared. "It could not withstand the seventy-pound push on the clutch. So I went to a place where they make braces for amputees and had a rig with chrome leg bracings set up for me. But that didn't work either. The boot came next. We wrapped it in fireproof material and stuck on the sandpaper. I barely passed the physical. The Sebring observers watched me like hawks when I practiced on the circuit. When they saw I could handle the car they passed me for the race, but it was close. I almost didn't make it."

Luckily for McQueen, the traditional Le Mans-type start (wherein drivers sprint across the track to their cars) was bypassed in 1970; a rolling start would be used, à la the Indy 500.

Using crutches, McQueen hobbled to his low white 908 and carefully eased his body into the narrow open cockpit. Inside, he fastened belts and adjusted his helmet.

A half-crippled movie actor was now ready to challenge Sebring's assembled aces.

Under a hot, muggy sun, in glittering rows of two, the cars got underway behind ex-world champion Phil Hill in the pace car, then cut loose at the flag in a released sea of roaring motors as 68 determined drivers jockeyed for the first turn at the end of the pit straight.

In speed and horsepower, McQueen's 3-liter 908 Porsche Spyder was simply no match for the factory-prepared 5-liter 512 Ferraris or the fantastic 4.5-liter 917 Porsches. Even in McQueen's 3-liter class, the Matra 650's, Alfa T-33's and the 312 Ferraris could potentially outgun the 908. Speed would not win the day for McQueen and Revson.

"We had determined to let the rabbits run," said Steve. "We were counting on the fact that many of the larger, faster machines would eliminate themselves in a twelve-hour grind by pushing too hard from the outset. Our plan was to stick to a safe, steady pace, to keep the car in good shape, then to make our strongest bid in the closing hours. Which meant that *smooth* driving, for us, was far more important than fast driving."

A two-car tangle directly behind the 908 on the first lap startled McQueen, but he maintained his pace, running in seventeenth position as the field began stringing out.

The race leaders were already pulling well ahead of the main pack, as Mario Andretti in a fierce red 512 Ferrari battled Jo Siffert's 917 Porsche, both of them challenged by Vic Elford in another savagely fast 917.

An hour passed on the official timing clock. Eleven to go.

Into the second hour, under the broiling Florida sun, tightly strapped in the 908's snug cockpit, McQueen threaded his way around the five-mile-plus Sebring circuit; he passed slower Fiats and Lancias, slipped the Porsche through the tricky Esses, downshifted for the hairpin, gunned along the straights, bumping over the rutted, broken runways—smoothly feeding power to the fuel-injected engine, learning to read each uneven stretch of grass-tufted concrete and raw blacktop.

"Toward the end of the second hour the pain from my left leg was really getting bad," he admitted. "I didn't want to hand over to Pete until I'd done my full two hours, but the pain was messing up my concentration. In a race, particularly a long-endurance race such as Sebring, concentration is everything. You can't let your mind wander. You must keep mentally alert each second you're out there. If you don't, you end up making a serious mistake, which might prove fatal. So I kept trying to tighten my concentration, knowing I didn't have long to go."

Still, almost despite himself, Steve could not help thinking of the cycle race at Elsinore two weeks before and of the wild spill which had shattered his foot. He'd been lucky. It could have been a lot worse. . . .

The cycle course was a killer. It began on a winding, paved road, zigzagged onto a half mile of dirt, spanned two drainage ditches, ran along more pavement into choppy

12

terrain, began alternating between desert-type trails, sand washes and graded dirt, narrowed to a single-lane mountain road flanked by a rock wall and a 500-foot plunge, dipped into the town of Elsinore, switched and swerved through the paved city streets onto steel railheads as it crossed train tracks into a 180-degree hairpin, whipped past the park into some tricky esses—and finally led back to the winding paved road again. Ten laps of this for 100 miles, with crowds pressing in every foot of the way.

Crowds made the third annual Lake Elsinore Grand Prix a nightmare for its riders: A seething, uncontrollable mass of 40,000 people jammed the California circuit, many of them standing or sitting on curbs inches away from the roaring cycles. A blown tire, an oil skid, a single mistake—and a cycle would be into the crowd. A woman had already been hit by cyclist Malcolm Smith early in the going. She was not badly injured, but Smith was out of the race.

For Steve McQueen, hunched low over the bars of his fast Motocross Husky, feeding power into the 405-cc engine, Elsinore was simply another contest which fired his eye and charged his blood.

"I *almost* ran a 500-cc Husky in this one," said Steve. "Bud Ekins and I took the Husky out for practice over the Mint 400 circuit, near Vegas, and it was a smooth bike, really good on the rocks. It was set up to handle rough terrain and was very fast. But it was a bit too heavy, so I decided to go with the 405. But I had to be careful, because a 405 Husqvarna kind of *explodes* under you if you feed in too much power. When you let it go on pavement it grabs traction so fast you can end up on the phone wires! You've got to respect it. It's not a bike to take for granted."

In the 500-cycle field over the rugged 10-mile circuit, McQueen took just three laps to work his way forward,

13

running with the leaders, passing many faster competitors.

Trouble was waiting in the fourth lap.

Steve was coming swiftly out of a wash under a bridge. A road dip lay ahead. It was deeper than he'd expected it to be, chopped up by the wheels of other riders, and he should have geared down to third for it. But he was counting on racer's skill to get him through. It didn't. The Husky struck the dip, was airborne, banged down again, twisting violently. McQueen was thrown over the bars into the crowd. Two spectators were knocked down.

The fall broke his left foot in six places.

"But I had my juice up," said Steve. "I'd been havin' a good go and the bike was okay, so I got back on board and ran the last six laps with my busted foot. Which was all right on the faster portions, when I could use the seat, but when I had to stand on the pegs through the rougher sections . . . well, that was kinda hard on me. Anyhow, they told me I finished sixth, but I messed up my foot a little doing it."

In McQueen's mind, the roar of racing cycles faded into the deeper jungle-cat roar of racing sports cars as the twelve hours of Sebring ground on into the heat of a muggy Florida afternoon.

Steve's performance was now being affected by the intense pain from his throbbing left foot. ("I was getting weird flashes and dingy vision on the straights. And I was so hot my skin just seemed to be burning up. I knew I had to bring in the 908—so I did, pitting for fuel and a driver change. Pete asked how things were and I assured him everything was okay, that the Porsche was running great. Which was true. I just didn't bother to mention how *I* was!")

While Revson drove, Steve had his foot packed in ice, drank "about a gallon of water," had the cast retaped and got some needed rest. ("As far as pain was concerned, the worst was over.")

Sebring, as usual, was stressing man and machine to the utmost: an MGB had lost a wheel and flipped on the high-speed sweeper coming off the pit straight; into the third hour—with the 908 running well in tenth, while three 512 Ferraris contested the lead—Sam Posey's 512 was hit by a Lancia in a metal-rending five-car crash near the hairpin. Elford's 917 Porsche was caught in the tangle, shedding a wheel. Posey and Elford were no longer potential winners. And by the fifth hour another accident involved Chuck Parsons in his 312 Ferrari. He'd entered the long bend past the Esses, throttling up to 140, when he realized that a course worker was on the track, picking up debris. Parsons tried to avoid contact, but the side of the Ferrari clipped the worker in passing; the man survived with a badly slashed leg.

Six hours. The sun sliding down the baked Florida sky, the crowd excited and murmuring as the halftime results were posted. The Revson/McQueen plan was paying off: with half of the race behind them, the pair had brought the white 908 into serious contention. They were running first in class and fourth overall!

Only three cars were ahead of the humming 908—the powerful trio of 512 factory Ferraris, with Andretti pacing the lot.

"Our situation improved even more shortly after halftime," said Steve, "when the Jackie Ickx Ferrari ran into problems."

Six hours of competition had ended the red car's run; a blown head gasket put Ickx out of the race. And Dan Gurney, another major threat to the 908, had dropped well back with a sour engine.

Night closed over the Sebring airport circuit; cars ripped past the stands along the pit straight in slashes of light and sound. Tension mounted. Each pit manager held the same question in mind: Will our car hold out to the end?

"At nine hours, the three-quarter mark," said McQueen,

"the T-33 Alfa of Masten Gregory had taken over third. Andretti still led, followed by Pedro Rodriguez in the 917 Porsche. Then we were in there in fourth. Ferrari, Porsche, Alfa and Porsche. Our 908 was running clock-smooth, and the leg pain wasn't bad by then. In fact, my lap times had picked up after dark; I had a much firmer grasp of the course, and of how hard I could take each of the turns. We were pushing it now, but being careful with things, not overstraining the car. It was just as we'd figured—the rabbits were tiring."

With two hours to go, the Alfa fell back—and the Rodriguez Porsche was also slowing. The McQueen/Revson 908 advanced two more positions into an astonishing second overall behind the big Andretti/Marzario Ferrari.

A blare of loudspeakers drew the exhausted crowd to the fence line; eyes strained the course for sight of the leaders. Andretti's car was out! At ten and a half hours, the leading Ferrari had coasted to a stop with a ruined transmission.

"For a crazy while there it looked as if we might take home the overall win," recalled McQueen. "Pete was driving the final double shift, doing great—but we couldn't quite pull it off."

Revson was passed by the Rodriguez/Siffert 917, and with less than an hour remaining, the fourth-running 512 Ferrari, driven by Vacarella, was called into the pits and a driver change was made: Andretti took over. Driving at the full range of his talent, and with a fast car under his throttle foot, Andretti instantly began closing on the two Porsches. With 22 minutes left on the clock he slammed the Italian machine past Revson to regain the lead (as the Rodriguez/Siffert 917 suddenly expired with front-wheel failure).

Revson kept after Mario, but the more powerful 512 soon opened a solid 30-second lead. There seemed no chance whatever that the 908 could catch Andretti in the closing minutes.

Another blare of loudspeakers! Andretti was slowing, his engine missing, sputtering. He was running out of gas—and on the next-to-last lap! The crowd began shouting; photographers were running toward the McQueen pits.

"You've won it!" yelled a mechanic, slapping Steve on the back.

"Not yet, not yet!" he snapped. "It isn't over yet."

He was correct. Andretti had switched to the reserve tank and rolled into the Ferrari pits. In a frantic few seconds he was away with gas enough to finish.

Revson, his lights slashing the circuit, was driving all-out in the ghost-white 908, as Mario blasted the big red car back into action.

Pete had won back several vital seconds, but the gap was too great. And the 908 just did not possess enough raw power to overcome the fire of Ferrari and the fully extended talent of Mario Andretti. In what was the closest finish in Sebring's two decades of international racing, Andretti swept under the checker to cinch the overall prize by a shade over 22 seconds.

McQueen and Revson had brilliantly won their 3-liter prototype class, finishing a full lap ahead of the third-place Gregory/Hazemans T-33 Alfa. Steve's most valued cup, however, was his alone: the Hayden Williams Sportsmanship Trophy awarded him for his incredible leg-in-a-cast driving performance of twelve exhausting hours of speed.

Andretti was grateful to have pulled off the overall win. "I never drove so hard in my life, not even when I won Indy. This was the toughest race I've run and I'm lucky to have taken it in those final minutes."

McQueen admitted, "We never really expected anything

like this." The crowd surged in and threatened to trample down a chain-link fence. Could Steve try to calm them?

He stood atop a truck and raised his hand in the peace sign. They quieted as he gestured them back. The leg ached, but he smiled broadly. Joy overcame pain, and his joy was great.

The old, soon-to-be-retired Sebring circuit was to host one final event (in March, 1971) before being replaced as a world racing site. Many of the greatest automotive battles of the postwar decades had been fought here, but there was never a closer finish in Sebring's twenty-one-year history than in this astonishing contest when one of the sport's champion drivers in a powerful factory Ferrari barely edged out the privately entered 908 of a lame film star. No script writer could have improved on Sebring, 1970.

For Steve McQueen this race mirrored his own dramatic life story in which he had fought his way up from behind, against tremendous odds, to reach the winner's circle.

18

2

A REBEL ON THE RUN

His root beginnings were harsh. The scars from his formative years have never left him. And the pain came early. . . .

Steve was just six months old when his father walked out for good after a bitter quarrel. William McQueen was a man who liked to keep on the move on the ground and off it. Bill was a stunt pilot, handling spit-and-polish crates, a roving country-fair barnstormer who'd happily risk his neck for a Sunday carnival crowd. He did barrel rolls and Immelmanns, looped and dived for air circus fans. Between shows, he'd hedge-hop the States, crop-dusting for his gas and the price of a meal.

Bill met a pretty teen-age girl, Julian Crawford, while he was in St. Louis, married her there, then moved on to Indiana where their son was born. But family life trapped him. He was a man who hated to be tied to one town, a man basically unsuited to marriage and responsibilities. He rejected his infant son and teen-age wife one bitter afternoon in September, 1930. William McQueen walked out of their lives, never to return.

"I didn't know much about my father," said Steve, "except that he must have had a weird sense of humor, naming me after Steve Hall, a one-armed bookie pal of his. Not many fathers name their sons after one-armed bookies!"

On March 24, 1930, he'd been born Terrence Steven McQueen at Beech Grove Hospital in a suburb of Indianapolis. His mother, Julian Crawford McQueen, was only nineteen at his birth, a girl who was almost as uncertain in her new parental role as her vagabond husband had been in his. Unable to face the complex problems of raising a son alone, the deserted mother took baby Steve to his Uncle Claude W. Thompson in Slater, Missouri, a small farming community in Saline County, near the Missouri River, about sixty miles east of Kansas City.

The boy's unhappy mother soon embarked for a new life in the big cities, leaving Steve to grow up with Thompson and his wife. "Uncle Claude was a good man," claimed McQueen. "I learned a lot from him. He was very strong, very fair. And he loved the land, always."

One of Steve's first vivid memories concerns the fast tricycle his Uncle Claude bought him when he was four. He'd take it to the top of a local hill and pedal furiously down the grade, pretending he was winning a race. Even at this very early age, speed fascinated and lured Steve McQueen.

At five he suffered a serious mastoid infection, an inflammation of the temporal bone located behind his left ear. No antibiotics were available in 1935 and the infection spread to the middle ear before it was controlled. (The deafness McQueen now suffers in this ear first began with the mastoid trouble.)

Life in rural Missouri appealed to the boy. Sports-minded from the outset, Steve enjoyed fishing the clear streams and creeks, playing ball in the open field behind the schoolhouse, riding a neighbor's pony around the pasture. Working on his uncle's farm toughened his young body, and he acquired his lasting love for the land, a joy *in* the earth and *of* the earth.

Julian McQueen had now become Mrs. Berri—and Steve met his new stepfather when he joined his mother in California. The relationship was a cold one; no warmth was struck between the boy and the man. "We didn't like each other," admitted Steve. "There was tension from the first moment I shook his hand."

Steve soon came to resent his stepfather's stern disciplinary nature and was in turn resented for his strong-minded individualism and stubbornness. At twelve Steve was already "a car nut." He put together a hot rod with the help of an older buddy. They successfully joined a Model-A frame with a Ford 60 engine, producing a potent street machine.

"It had an Edelbrock manifold," recalled Steve. "We could accelerate with a J-2 Allard which was *the* going sports car around there at the time. Our rod didn't handle for beans, but when the engine stayed together that machine had *stark* acceleration. It was a real jumper."

As he entered his adolescent years Steve grew more restless and rebellious; he felt unloved, unwanted. The warming influence of his uncle was replaced by anxiety and a desperate sense of personal desolation. He felt that his mother had deserted him in Missouri as his father had deserted him in Indiana. And now she seemed to side with his stepfather against him.

In an attempt to win attention Steve began to break the law. When his stepfather found that Steve had been involved in several minor thefts he administered a severe beating. More beatings followed—and the boy retaliated with fresh acts of rebellion.

Finally, when Steve was just six months past his fourteenth birthday, the situation reached a critical stage.

"I want him out of this house!" shouted his stepfather.

"But where can he go?" Steve's mother asked. "We have nowhere to send him."

"Send him to a place where they'll teach him some discipline. And do it *now*!"

Declaring her son "incorrigible," Julian enrolled him, as Steve Berri, at the California Junior Boys Republic at Chino. Within three months he'd run away, was brought back, punished and assigned laundry duty at the corrective institution.

Frank Graves, who was then principal at the Boys Republic, admitted that young McQueen was something of a problem. "He was sour, quiet, a rebel who didn't like anything or anybody. Yet I could see he was intelligent and terribly deprived. He was tough to handle and ran away twice between February, 1945, and April of the following year. His mother would find him and bring him back. He settled down a bit after the second runaway attempt."

Steve credited the change in his basic attitude to a concerned counselor who took a close personal interest in him. "This man helped me find myself," Steve said. "For the first time in my life I began to think of myself as *worth* saving. Living began to make a little sense. I learned self-discipline, learned that the one who benefitted most from it was me. And I learned to take pride in something I could do with my hands."

McQueen became expert at fashioning Christmas wreaths which were sold each holiday season to help finance the school, and he also worked with wood and metal in the shop. He made friends among the boys, shared their jokes and troubles. With a ninth-grade education,

Steve left the institution at Chino a month after his sixteenth birthday to join his mother in New York in April, 1946.

"But we didn't stay together for long," he said. "I had a yen to cut loose, to see the world."

He signed as ordinary seaman aboard a Greek oil tanker bound for foreign shores but grew tired of tasteless deck chow and jumped ship. Steve earned meals doing carpentry work and delivering groceries, then made his way to Texas. ("The oil fields needed grouts so I became one!") As a grout, or common laborer, he worked various oil rigs near Waco and Corpus Christi.

Staying loose, he joined a traveling carnival as a barker and left it at Ottawa to become a "tree-topper" in a Canadian lumber camp. The job was rough and dangerous, but McQueen adapted to it, winning the crew's respect.

In April, 1947, having turned seventeen that March, he enlisted in the Marine Corps for a three-year stint. Military life didn't appeal to the rebel in him; chafing under camp discipline, he stretched a weekend pass into a three-week vacation leave—and upon his return was promptly thrown into the brig. ("They busted me down from PFC to private about seven times!")

His salvation came when he was assigned to the tank corps as a mechanic-driver. "We had this old tank," said McQueen, "and I thought it could be souped up. So a couple of the guys and me, we really worked it over, porting and milling the heads, fooling around with the timing and carburation. The whole bit. Well, on the day we finished, we took it out for a timed run. And the laugh was on us; it didn't go *any* faster. I found out the hard way that you can't soup a tank, though we sure bruised our knuckles tryin' to!"

Steve never seemed to get enough to eat as a Marine. At least that's the way he remembers it. His appetite spurred him into another wild escapade during this period.

McQueen's outfit was moved to Labrador for cold-weather amphibious exercises, and rations were cut in keeping with the spirit of the situation. On emergency rations, Steve found himself "half-starved and always thinking about food."

He was ordered to the wharf to help unload a landing craft full of food for the officers' mess. Steve jumped into an Amtrac and hustled down to the boat. During the unloading operation he helped himself to several cans of beans which he stowed carefully away in the Amtrac for future feasts.

"The trouble was," said Steve, "that the cans were all ice cold. I came up with a way to heat them. I got my crew chief to rev up the Amtrac's engine while I held a can of beans over the hot exhaust. This went on for about four minutes, which would have been fine except that I'd forgotten to *open* the can. Suddenly, there was this tremendous explosion. It blew beans over everything —tents, jeeps, radar equipment, everything. And for about the next week I'd go by an officer and salute him and he'd have a bean stuck on his helmet. I had a lot of trouble keeping a straight face down there in Labrador."

Steve's hitch ended when he was honorably discharged from the corps at Camp Lejeune in North Carolina in April, 1950, just three years from the day he'd enlisted. He was twenty and ready for fresh adventure.

With back pay bulging his pockets, McQueen met a girl from Myrtle Beach, South Carolina, and decided to visit her town. He spent a month there, as well as most of his back pay.

"We ran around with a young crowd of college kids," he recalled. "Here I was, going over to fancy apartments and homes for dinner, getting dressed up for dates, going to dances. . . . Everybody was open and friendly. I'd never had this kind of life before. I fell into it the way you fall into a dream."

But the social dream ended abruptly with the last of his cash, and Steve thumbed his way to New York, where he rented a cold-water walk-up in Greenwich Village for nineteen dollars a month.

The Village became his turf; it fascinated him with its raw vitality and kinetic atmosphere of "things happening." He sensed a future here, a way to achievement. . . .

At this point in his unsettled life Steve had no idea what he wanted as a career. He was totally directionless, willing to "try anything that would pay the rent and put some food in my stomach."

Jobs were plentiful for a tough-bodied youngster who didn't mind sweating for a dollar. McQueen worked as a taxi mechanic, carried radiators out of condemned buildings, sold ball-point pens, trimmed leather for a sandalmaker, delivered radios and TV sets and even tried his skill at assembling artificial flowers "in a smelly little dark cellar on Third Avenue."

Between jobs he found a cook in a small restaurant who would stake him for meals. "He would trust me up to thirty bucks worth of veal cutlets and beer. And he gave me a nickname—Desperado. Which I *was* in those days."

Steve's conscience finally made him quit a job as a door-to-door salesman. ("I felt like a shark going into those poor family homes and talking them into encyclopedias.")

That winter, in order to escape the freezing winds of New York, Steve and a pal bummed their way to Florida, where McQueen worked as a beach boy for a Miami hotel, "serving drinks and chasing after cigarettes while I got myself a suntan and learned to skin-dive." The diving was costly to his hearing: Water pressure punctured his left eardrum.

Back in New York he obtained part-time work as a night bartender. During daylight hours he was taking an on-the-job course in tile-setting. ("I'd found out that a tile man, if he's really skilled, could earn pretty good money. So I kind of set my sights on becoming a professional tile-setter. I even got a crazy idea about going to Spain, where there's lots of tile, and studying there.")

Speed and hot engines were still prime enthusiasms, and by the fall of 1951 he'd saved enough to buy a battered cycle with a sidecar which he proudly tooled around the Village. ("My dates rode in the sidecar.")

"It was my first bike and I loved it," admitted Steve. "But I was going with this girl who began to hate that cycle—just hated riding in the bumpy sidecar. She told me, 'Either the cycle goes or I go!' Well, there was no contest. *She* went."

Steve found a new girl, a young actress who told him she thought he had a natural stage presence.

"What's that mean?" he wanted to know.

"It means I think you could be an actor with some training. Want to see what acting's all about?"

Amused and curious, Steve accompanied her to an afternoon acting class, where he met Sanford Meisner, director of the Neighborhood Playhouse. He asked McQueen to read from a script and liked what he heard. He offered to take Steve on as a student.

"I knew he was an original," said Meisner. "He was both tough and childlike, as if he'd been through everything but had preserved a certain basic innocence."

McQueen accepted Meisner's offer and enrolled on the GI Bill. But acting was totally foreign to him and he was uncomfortable and nervous. The rebel in him asserted itself as a means of defense.

His voice teacher, Carol Veazie, had trouble with Steve: "In the beginning he was openly skeptical about acting and about any talent he might possess. He had a 'show me' attitude, was short-tempered and would prove his contempt by going to sleep in class."

But she did not give up on Steve. She was determined to break through, and she did. The breaking point came when

26

she forced him to listen to his voice on tape. "I guess Steve realized how bad he really was, because from that day forward he started trying."

With characteristic single-minded determination, which would be typical of him throughout his professional life, young McQueen attacked the mechanics of drama.

"If I was supposed to show up with two improvisations I'd show up with five," he said. "I really threw myself into the thing. And when training at the Playhouse got too expensive I got an after-hours job driving a Post Office truck to pay for my classes. I'd start out in the truck at seven, drive all night, then be at acting class the next morning. This went on for six months. The routine almost killed me, but it was worth the effort. After those six months I'd learned enough about acting to win a scholarship."

Meanwhile, having sold his sidecar rig, Steve had purchased a used K-model Harley and had hopped up the cycle's power plant. He learned to handle it at speed on New York's West Side Highway, then began racing weekends in Long Island City, dragging with other serious bikers for cash.

"It wasn't exactly safe," he admitted. "But I was able to take home close to a hundred dollars per weekend, which suddenly made living a lot easier."

His acting scholarship took him through courses at the Uta Hagen/Herbert Berghof Drama School, and early in 1952 Steve made his pro stage debut in a modest production on Second Avenue, delivering a single line of dialogue, "Nothing will help." In Yiddish.

"My roommate, a logger, helped me land the part," said Steve. "His sister was an actress and she talked them into hiring me. But I got fired after just four performances!"

A much more substantial role in a summer stock production of *Peg O' My Heart* (with Margaret O'Brien) failed to boost McQueen's shaky status. Steve was told by a disgruntled fellow actor: "I want you to know your acting is downright embarrassing."

But Steve kept improving. The strong competitive drive which was a vital part of his nature carried him into a Rochester Stock Company production of *Member of the Wedding,* starring the great Ethel Waters. He next embarked on a road version of *Time Out for Ginger*—where he found his first sports car in Columbus, Ohio, while touring with the play.

"I wasn't making much from my acting," said Steve, "but I was playing poker every night and winning. I'd learned to play a fair hand in the service. I found this sweet little British sports job, an MG-TC, which had a $750 price tag on it. I put down $450 out of my poker winnings—and I told the owner I'd send more money from each overnight stop we made. Which I did. It was finally delivered to me in Chicago. That's when I asked for a raise and got booted out of the play. So I jumped into my MG and drove it all the way back to New York."

Steve soon discovered that the upkeep on a used sports car can be alarmingly high. "I sold it after three axles broke and the spokes kept shredding out of those big wheels. I decided to stick with cycles for a while."

Slowly, role by role, Steve worked his way toward full professionalism. During the next two seasons he snagged minor jobs in television (on *U. S. Steel Hour* and the *Armstrong Circle Theater*) and garnered his first solid recognition with a memorable performance in a televised *Studio One* drama, *The Shrivington Raiders.*

However, the major triumph of this period came when Steve auditioned for the coveted Actors Studio. Of the two thousand applicants that year, McQueen was one of five chosen for admission. He had conclusively demonstrated his potential, but, as he declared, "potential doesn't pay your bills."

During his tenure of study at the Actors Studio

(extending into 1956) McQueen worked at a variety of odd jobs around Manhattan and added to his dramatic credits by co-starring with Gary Merrill in a Broadway production of *The Gap*.

As winter closed over the city Steve worked the Manhattan docks for three cold months, unloading freight from cargo ships along the Hudson. It was rugged and exhausting; the wind off the river cut into his body—and a snarling foreman continually made acid remarks about actors who tried to be freight handlers. On more than one occasion they almost came to blows. ("But I had to put food in my mouth, so I survived. I had a strong back, which helped. Any way you figure it, though, that was one lousy job!")

But Steve's first real break was due. In the late summer of 1956 he auditioned to replace Ben Gazzara as the star of the hit Broadway drama *A Hatful of Rain*.

"He was an eager kid, shy and offbeat," recalled director Frank Corsaro. "He seemed so naïve, we called him Cornflake. But he won the part."

Steve felt lacking in the role. "I didn't have Ben's technical facility," he said. "Still, I made the most of what I had. I remember there was one scene in the play in which the character was supposed to be delirious. Each night I did this scene I got more and more depressed. For a while I got so bugged I couldn't eat and began losing weight. The lines were getting to me. But we had a three-month run, and I eventually snapped myself out of it and got some good notices."

At the age of twenty-six Steve McQueen had made his professional breakthrough: He was starring, to critical praise, in a solid Broadway hit.

Thanks to that same play, he was about to make an equally meaningful breakthrough in his personal life: He was about to meet a girl named Neile.

3

BOUNTY HUNTING IN HOLLYWOOD

Neile Adams had been born in the Philippines, in Manila. Her father, Joseph Adams, was British; her mother, Carmen Salvador, was Spanish. They separated when she was very young, and she never really knew her father. Neile led a sheltered childhood, receiving her education in a convent. When the Japanese invaded the Philippines she worked for guerrilla forces as a messenger until she was captured and placed in a concentration camp where she spent a year and a half as a prisoner under brutally severe conditions. At war's end she moved with her mother to New York, where she attended a girls' boarding school in Connecticut. Here she learned to dance, winning a scholarship at Katherine Dunham's. Her petite, dark-haired beauty, combined with a natural grace and a sweet singing voice, gained her a part in *Kismet*, and within two years she'd been picked to replace the Broadway star of *Pajama Game*. Neile was superb in the part, an overnight sensation.

Which is when she entered the life of Steve McQueen, then starring in *Hatful of Rain*.

He was having dinner with an actor-pal at Downey's, a favorite show business spot, when Neile walked in with her date of the evening. McQueen vividly recalled the moment: "Here was this girl with smooth tan skin and dancer's legs and big white teeth walking by our table in a tight skirt. I was so shook I dropped a forkful of spaghetti in my lap."

Steve promptly introduced himself and asked Neile for a date. She accepted, having no idea of the nature of a McQueen date.

"I was startled when he showed up on a motorcycle," she admitted. "When he told me to hop aboard I was half terrified. I'd never ridden a cycle—but it was fun. The following Sunday we went to New Jersey for a picnic, which was lovely. We ate with some other friends of Steve's who'd all arrived on their cycles, and on the way back, coming down this winding road, they all started racing each other. The sparks were flying off the foot pegs and I was hanging onto Steve. . . . Well, he won. He always won. Twenty-five dollars one time, a hundred the next. That's what supported him. That and poker. He invited me to a lot of picnics after that first one, and I'd always find myself in the middle of a race. Once I burned my leg on the exhaust pipe. He was a wild man come into my life. A delightful wild man."

Claimed Steve: "I showed her a new way of life. No getting dressed up, no makeup, no fancy stockings, no big parties. . . . Just long rides into the country—the two of us alone on a fast bike."

When their dates continued, Neile's agent became furious. "You're a dancer," he yelled at her. "You'll break a leg on those crazy cycles. And you can't dance in a cast!"

But Neile ignored all warnings; their relationship

deepened when she found out about Steve's deprived, loveless childhood.

"We had both come from broken homes," she related. "That gave us a bond. He was so tied into himself. Love and hope had no meaning for him. He didn't know about love because no one had ever loved him, and he didn't believe in hope because no one had ever given him any. Hope was a trick people used to soften you up, and he wanted to stay tough. He was sure that life was dog-eat-dog.

"Steve had never really trusted any woman before I came along, not even his mother. But, slowly, he began to trust me. I sensed this desperate *need* in him. That's how it began—and it just kept building."

The intensity of their relationship surprised McQueen; he had not expected to become so deeply involved with this girl. When he left *Hatful of Rain* in October he took off with two cycle buddies for a visit to Cuba. He needed some time away from Neile "to get things straight in my head." Cuba was a fine excuse.

"I had my 650 BSA and my buddies each had their rigs—a one-lung Norton Manx and a 500 BMW—and we all cycled down to Key West and took the TMT ferry across to Havana. Castro and Batista were shootin' at each other about then, and things were a little tense. I tried to sell a guy some cigarettes and got thrown in jail on a charge of pushing American contraband. I wired Neile for the money I needed to get sprung, but she was mad at me for leavin' her in New York and said no. Ended up selling my crash helmet and some parts off the BSA to bail myself out of there and get back home."

Back in Manhattan, with the Cuban adventure behind him, he got his first movie role—a walk-on in the Robert Wise production *Somebody Up There Likes Me*, which starred Paul Newman. Steve wore a beany and had a single line of dialogue to deliver.

McQueen has often been compared in his life-style and tough-tender acting technique to the late James Dean. Both had attended Actors Studio, both raced street cycles, both were in their twenties. It is ironic that Steve would get his first film assignment in the picture in which Dean was to star. (Newman had replaced Jimmy in the role of boxer Rocky Marciano after the young actor was killed in a racing Porsche Spyder late in 1955.)

Neile got a call to fly to California on a film, and Steve followed soon after. He was now sure that he wanted to marry her.

"It was all pretty frantic," said Neile. "My mother considered Steve to be some kind of bike bum and wouldn't have a thing to do with him. And my Coast agent told me to forget him, that he had no future in Hollywood. But when he asked me to be his wife I couldn't say no. We *needed* each other."

In November, 1956, Steve bought a forty-dollar wedding ring, borrowed a suit from a friend, and rented a Ford Thunderbird for their wedding trip. They planned to marry at the San Juan Capistrano Mission but were refused permission on the basis of their not being members of the local parish.

Steve was mad. He gunned the T-Bird onto the highway in a shower of gravel, accelerating briskly away. Red lights flashed behind him. A pair of state troopers roared up on the Thunderbird.

"All right, buddy, what's the rush?"

Steve shrugged. "No rush. We just tried to get married and they wouldn't let us. Is it a crime to want to get married?"

After a brief discussion (part of which involved certain technical details relating to police cycles *vs*. street cycles) the two officers expressed sympathy for the frustrated couple.

"Listen," one of them said, "I know a Lutheran minister

in San Clemente. Maybe he'll open his church for you and perform the service. Want me to call him?"

"Sure do!" said Steve.

Escorted by the police, McQueen happily motored up the Coast to a small white Lutheran church in San Clemente. He and Neile were married there, with the two state troopers standing by as witnesses.

"It was kind of spooky," admitted McQueen, in recalling the ceremony. "Here we were getting hitched with those two big cops standing right behind us with their belted pistols and all. It felt like a shotgun wedding!"

Their Mexican honeymoon was cut short by Neile's screen role in *This Could Be the Night* and a hurried flight to New York for a television guest shot.

Steve got work in St. Louis on two films locationing in that city. He played a Jewish lawyer in *Never Love a Stranger* and a local youth captured by bank robbers in *The Great St. Louis Bank Robbery*. Both pictures were undistinguished "quickies."

Meanwhile, Neile had flown to Las Vegas to fulfill her contract as a singer/dancer at the Tropicana. The job was worth $1,500 a week, and she remained there through 1957.

"We didn't like being separated," said Neile. "Steve would fly in every weekend from St. Louis to be with me. He even bought me a Corvette and tried to teach me to drive."

The lessons were not altogether successful: Neile wrecked the Corvette—and all but wrecked their marriage during the same period.

"Our big problem was money," she explained. "By the end of 1957 I'd made about fifty thousand dollars to his six thousand, and I bought myself a new Lincoln to replace the Corvette. This difference in our earnings really bugged Steve. His pride was very much involved. We'd yell at each

34

other over the phone. He felt lacking in terms of career, and this caused tension, arguments."

Early in 1958 Neile quit her job in Vegas and they rented a modest house in North Hollywood while Steve looked for film work.

"I didn't find anything for a while," he said. "Which meant I had to keep flying back East to take shots at TV roles. I played a lot of killers and mixed-up delinquents."

Finally he snagged a starring role in a low-budget science fiction horror film, *The Blob*, in which he portrayed a teen-ager who defeated a gooey menace from outer space. This picture, which cost under $150,000 to produce, grossed four million dollars. (Steve's fee was a flat $3,000, with no percentages.)

Discouraged and disgusted, McQueen made another run back to New York for more television work. He received a call from a West Coast agent, asking him to return to Hollywood.

"It was for TV, and I almost didn't go," said Steve. "It sounded no better than what I was already doing back East. But I went—and that was the beginning of *Wanted—Dead or Alive*."

The route leading to what was to become a smash-hit TV series was complex: Cy Marsh, a local Hollywood agent, had talked writer/producer Frank Gruber into hiring McQueen for a segment of Gruber's new Western series, *Wells Fargo*—three days' work at a fee of $400. But when he saw him, the producer didn't like McQueen. He felt that his five-foot-ten-inch height was a problem.

"This guy is too short," Gruber complained. "Viewers won't buy him for a Western. They like tall heroes."

At this same time (the fall of 1958), Vincent Fennelly, producer of *Trackdown,* another Western series, needed an actor to play the part of a bounty hunter in one of the televised segments. McQueen auditioned for the part.

Fennelly took him on—for the same reasons Gruber had rejected him: He was small; viewers would root for him against bigger bad guys.

"I wasn't very happy about the thing," said McQueen. "I had it pegged as just one more guest shot—although the idea of playing the part of a pro gunman who chases after outlaws for a price appealed to me."

The show was filmed, and Fennelly liked the segment enough to try it on CBS as the spinoff for a series he wanted to produce, *Wanted—Dead or Alive*. The network chiefs bought the idea. Suddenly Steve McQueen was the star of his own TV show!

"Here was this little guy," said Fennelly. "Sort of an underdog. Offbeat, with a kind of animal instinct. He wasn't a pretty boy; he looked tough enough to be a professional hunter. There was menace behind his quick smile, a promise of violence. And it all came across on the TV screen. We knew we had something special here."

McQueen's initial contract called for him to receive $750 a week, and if the series clicked he would not have to keep flying back to New York in order to get work. This show represented, at last, a solid chance of success on the West Coast—meaning that he and Neile could settle down in California.

"I liked Josh Randall," said McQueen of the character he portrayed. "He was a lot like me—a loner who played his own game, made his own decisions. He was no hero strutting along with a badge pinned to his chest; he was a hired man doing a hired man's job for the money it paid him. I could identify with Randall, and I think the audience sensed that identification and responded to it."

Steve had strong ideas about just how Randall's character should be drawn, and he argued with the producer, directors and writers over what the bounty hunter would or would not do.

"They started to make a superman out of him," recalled

Steve. "They'd have three big, mean-looking heavies with guns coming down the street toward Randall, and the script had him facing them all, head-on, for a showdown. Now, that was phony and I knew it. Randall could handle one gunman, but he'd never be dumb enough to face three at once. It would be suicide, and he was a smart boy—too clever for this kind of grandstand play."

He made them change this kind of scene; he sweated and yelled and used his savvy to make Randall a believable character who might really survive in the Old West. ("I'd been kicked around enough in my life to know what it takes to survive.")

Steve won the battle. Randall would be played and written *his* way.

Josh Randall's weapon was one of the distinctive elements in the show; instead of packing a rifle and six-shooters, he carried a cut-down .40-40 carbine, a "mare's leg," which combined the punch of a rifle with the mobility and quickness of a handgun. Determined to master this odd weapon, Steve practiced drawing and firing it several hours each day for weeks. He became an expert with the gun, perfecting a swivel-fire method which delighted TV fans.

Randall's horse presented yet another challenge for McQueen. A bounty hunter, he knew, needed a tough, spirited mount. Instead, fearful of Steve's ability to ride, the studio had provided an animal who was, according to McQueen, "so slow they had to wheel him into a scene on roller skates."

Steve "fired" the tired beast after six segments and sought out a rancher-friend in the area who raised quarter horses.

"He had this black, with white stocking feet, which I liked," said McQueen. "He'd just been broken and still had plenty of fire. I got on and he bucked me right off. That did it. I took him."

The horse, whose name was Ringo, did not enjoy

working in television; the lights, cables, sets and crew members all annoyed him.

"The first week we used him he kicked out five set lights," Steve related. "He also bit the other horses and broke my big toe by stomping on it. Ole Ringo and me, we fought each other. He'd reach his head back to bite me and I'd lean in and punch him on the nose. This kind of thing went on for months, but I refused to replace him. I liked his style. He had nerve and wouldn't back down to anybody."

Wanted—Dead or Alive was a solid hit with viewers; they took to the knockabout manhunter on the feisty black horse, and the show provided Steve with a steady income for the first time in his career. He sold his cycle and bought two sports cars, a black 1,600-cc Porsche roadster (the Super Speedster model) and a sleek green magnesium-bodied XK-SS British racing Jaguar. "That Jag was unique right from the day I got it," said Steve. "It was a direct development of the D-Type Jag that won Le Mans four times and it was very fast and brutal. Due to a fire, the factory turned out only fifteen of these cars. As things broke on it, I fixed them. I reengineered the combustion chambers and the cams, worked over the oil sump and radiator and bushed the front end. I loved that ole Jag."

The torpedo-shaped machine naturally attracted police attention, and Steve found himself collecting speeding tickets at a truly unsettling rate. Early in 1959, when he and Neile were in the Jag on the way to Phoenix, McQueen "let it hang out past a hundred." The road was smooth and the green car moved over it at 110 . . . 115 . . . 120 . . . when a pair of red lights began blinking far behind them.

"Wow!" exclaimed Steve, looking back at the patrol car, "I can't afford another ticket. They'll take my license."

"But you *were* speeding," said Neile, who was six months pregnant with their first child.

"Trust me," Steve told her, braking the Jag as the patrol

38

car pulled up to them. He jumped out, ran back to the policemen.

"Listen, officer," Steve panted, "you've got to help us. My wife is on the point of having a baby. Every second counts! Can you lead us to a hospital?"

"Sure, buddy, just follow us!" declared the officer, gunning off ahead of Steve's Jag. Under full siren, they sped to the nearest emergency hospital. A nurse rushed out to help Neile inside.

"Think she'll be okay?" the policeman asked Steve.

"Sure. She'll be fine now. Thanks to you."

The officers shook hands with Steve and took off back down the highway. McQueen rushed after the nurse, caught her. "Mistake," he grinned. "My wife's okay. She's cool. We just made a little mistake."

The nurse looked stunned as he hustled an angry-looking Neile back to their car.

"She didn't speak to me for the rest of the day," said Steve. "But it worked. I *didn't* get a ticket."

McQueen was becoming interested in the local racing events sponsored by the California Sports Car Club, but his XK was too rare an item to risk competing in; the 1600 Super Porsche, however, was ideal.

Steve took the black Porsche up to Mulholland Drive, a long stretch of twisting asphalt roadway in the hills above Hollywood, and began to "shake down" the car. When this road was clear of traffic, late at night, he and a group of other sports car drivers staged impromptu races. Steve ran his 1600 against 300-SL Mercedes, Corvettes and faster Porsche Carreras. ("I had a special switch rigged for the dash which made it possible to snap off the light over my back license plate if a patrol car showed.")

McQueen learned enough about the dynamics of fast cornering on Mulholland to equip him for his first sports car race; he entered a club event in late May, 1959, at Santa Barbara.

"I was put into a novice race," he said. "We had a real mixture of cars, big and small, and I had no idea where I'd finish. The guys in the Corvettes didn't seem to know what to do with all the horsepower, but there were some hot little Oscas. . . . Anyhow, I remember storming off the line like mad, passing a lot of other Porsches and some Triumphs, not paying much attention to my revs—until, about four laps into the race, I suddenly found myself leading the field. Which shook me. Here I was skidding around the circuit between cars, going as deep into the turns as possible before braking, on the ragged edge all the way, and I thought, 'Man, what are you *doing* out here?' But I hung on and won. After that I was hooked. Winning gives you a very heady feeling."

Steve kept on winning with the 1600—at Del Mar and Willow Springs, often beating the faster Carrera Porsches. ("The Supers were a bit lighter and had a lot of low-end snap, while it took a Carrera longer to get the revs up. You could nail 'em on a short course.")

Ron Bucknum was then considered the fastest Porsche driver in his class, and he gave McQueen a hand up. ("Racing Ronnie was an education!") When Steve switched to the faster Carrera he had a little sign painted on the front of his car: "Lookin' for Ronnie."

Neile did not share her husband's elation with sports car competition; she was about to give birth to a daughter, and Steve had promised her he'd stop racing when the baby arrived. Terry Leslie McQueen was born that June, but Steve did not quit the fast cars. He felt compelled to stay with them.

"Racing was giving me a fresh identity," he explained. "I was no longer just an actor; I was a man who raced, and that was important to me—to have this separate identity."

He traded his Porsche to sportsman Jack Reddish for a Lotus Le Mans Mark XI and continued to compete. ("In that Lotus I really started to become competitive. I was

40

smoother, more relaxed; the rough edges had been knocked off my driving. I was beginning to find out what real sports car racing was all about.")

He was also finding out more about film acting with the aid of movie veteran Frank Sinatra, who backed Steve with director John Sturges for a pivotal role in his war film *Never So Few*. Steve played a con artist named Ringer in a zany, fast-paced performance which finally revealed his big-screen potential.

"Frank and I dug each other," said Steve. "For one thing, we both share a passion for firecrackers. When we found six hundred cherry bombs on the back lot at Metro it was like Chinese New Year!"

One afternoon, when Steve was dozing through a lull between scenes, Sinatra deftly inserted a small firecracker in Steve's ammo belt. "The thing went off and shot me about three feet into the air. So I grabbed one of the Tommy guns we were using and jammed in a full clip. Frank was walking away from me, laughing it up with some pals, when I yelled at him. He turned around and looked plenty startled when I let him have the full clip, zap-zap-zap-zap-. . . . Of course, the thing was loaded with blanks, but the effect was wild. I figured that evened the score."

Despite the fact that Steve got excellent critical notices for his work in *Never So Few*, he could not take advantage of them in terms of future film projects. His *Wanted* series was still in full swing.

"The Sinatra film had been more or less a vacation for me," he admitted. "I was soon back at the TV grind: up at five thirty, to the studio by six thirty, work all day on the set, home by nine thirty that night. People outside the industry have no idea how hard a series TV star works to fill up all that air time. We'd do up to four *Wanted* segs in three days. It was murder."

Sports car racing continued to provide Steve with an

escape from the tensions of the set—and McQueen entered his Le Mans Lotus in the Santa Barbara races that Labor Day weekend (1959). He put up a stubborn wheel-to-wheel battle with Lotus ace Frank Monise in another Mark XI, winding up Saturday's event just a split second behind him, "about six inches off his tailpipe!"

In Sunday's main event, still chasing Monise, Steve overextended himself, charging into the turn nine hairpin. ("I spun and killed the engine, which cost me the race.") Two cars had slipped past him and Steve finished in fourth place.

At Del Mar he made another mistake. "I was leading with the Lotus when I accidentally hit this switch on the dash which cut my power. It was an emergency fuel switch for changing tanks. As a result, the car just died on me. I was embarrassed about that, but I was still learning. Each time you race you learn more."

As a "lark," in 1960, Steve and Neile appeared together as an acting team on television. They did a Hitchcock segment and guested on the Bob Hope and Perry Como variety shows. Neile had more or less abandoned her career in favor of her husband's ("one actor in a family is enough!") and she appreciated the chance to show off her talents once again.

McQueen's *Wanted* was hotter than ever in national ratings, and his salary had jumped to $100,000 a year. He was able to break free of Josh Randall for one feature film that year, *The Magnificent Seven,* another Sturges production in which Steve played a key role as a Western gunman, one of seven men hired to save a village from Mexican bandits. Yul Brynner starred, a man who had no patience with supporting actors who gave him advice. Steve found this out when he attempted to explain to Brynner just how a pro gunman ties down his weapon.

A feud developed between the two actors, aided by the press. They quoted Steve: "I think, in this film, I represent a threat to Mr. Brynner. He doesn't ride very well and he doesn't know anything about quick draws and that kind of thing. Well, I know horses and guns. I'm in my element and he isn't. I guess I make him nervous."

McQueen also made his TV producers nervous. After *Seven*, upon resuming his bounty hunter role, he was asked to sell the Lotus. Which he did. He now had the added responsibility of a baby son—Chadwick Steven McQueen was born in December—plus a home to pay for on Solar Drive in Nichols Canyon.

"I got me a house on a hill, an old lady who loves me, two kids and plenty of fruit and nuts on the table," he told a reporter. "I'm cool, man. I can afford to quit racing for a while."

In April, 1961, after 117 segments, *Wanted—Dead or Alive* finally bit the dust. McQueen was free to accept film assignments. Josh Randall, the relentless bounty hunter, was to live only on reruns.

"Ole Josh gave me a start," said Steve. "I'm grateful to him for that. But he's behind me and now I can do some hunting on my own. And, man, I'm just starting on the trail."

4

ON THE WAY TO THE TOP

For a change of pace, after the hard-boiled realism of the *Wanted* scripts, Steve signed for a lightweight comedy, *The Honeymoon Machine*. He played a crew-cut Navy lieutenant who rigs an electronic computer to win at roulette. Unhappily, the production was thin and labored in its humor; during its MGM executive preview Steve walked out, unable to endure his self-conscious screen mugging.

"I'd made seven films up to then," he said, "and only one, the Sturges Western, was any good. I decided to try doing one in Europe and accepted a role in *The War Lover*."

In this film Steve was a headstrong, gung-ho B-17 bomber pilot who betrays his best friend and dies in a crash at the picture's end. The role was essentially anti-hero and offbeat. Philip Leacock was the director, and Steve was to be based in London during the shooting schedule, with his co-starring salary set at $75,000.

"My agent had a special bit written into my contract," said Steve. "He had the studio agree to provide me with a limousine and chauffeur to get me to the set. But that wasn't my thing, and I told the studio people, 'Why not let me buy a small car and drive it myself?' This saved them money so they okayed the offer. As a result, I got me a twelve-speed, four-wheel-drive Land Rover, which I shipped back to California after the film was over. I came out ahead on the deal."

In Europe the racing fever struck again. Spectating at local events on circuits near London fired Steve with a desire to compete. The studio heads at Columbia had sternly warned him that if he *did* race and was seriously injured, he'd be sued for the production costs of *War Lover*. (Which could come to over two and a half million.)

McQueen stayed out of cars during the weekdays on the set, but each weekend he'd "wrangle a ride" at club events. He was fifth at Oulton Park, was an also-ran at Aintree, but took a solid third overall at Brands Hatch. His new-found friend, the great British champion Stirling Moss, helped Steve learn the fastest way around various circuits by driving just ahead and signaling with two fingers if the turn required second gear, three fingers for third gear, and so on.

It was at the Brands Hatch circuit that Steve got into trouble. "I was running in the wet with this Mini-Cooper S when a brake locked on me. This threw my car sideways as I was coming out of a fast turn, and I knew I couldn't hold the road. Not on a wet track."

A sports writer graphically described Steve's performance under stress: "As he hurtled downhill, off the road, McQueen did a superb job of propelling the Cooper between poles and metal signs that could have demolished it. He controlled the slide until the final instant, looped, and slammed the car at an angle into a dirt embankment. The Cooper snapped around like a top, whirling and bouncing, but miraculously did not turn over."

Steve had split his lower lip in the impact and worried about what the studio would do if he delayed production. He had close-ups due the following Monday. ("But the director saved the day by letting me do all my scenes in an oxygen mask in the cockpit, so everything was cool.")

Through his association with Moss, Steve had contacted John Cooper, head of the British Motor Corporation's racing team, and had purchased an 1,100-cc Formula Jr. Cooper (the same car BMC-driver Tony Maggs had driven in France for the team at Reims).

In addition to his Land Rover, Steve managed to have the fast British racing machine shipped back to the States, with the idea of competing in the Cooper on the West Coast.

The ex-poor boy from Missouri had his own personal valet while he was in London. ("He made me kinda jumpy, but he came with the fancy house we rented there.") The ornate four-story town house in Chester Square belonged to diplomat Lord Russell and was provided for McQueen after he had been asked to vacate his suite at the Savoy.

"I'd had a few racing pals up to my rooms in the hotel," explained Steve. "We were scrambling eggs over a hot plate—which the management frowns on—when a curtain caught fire. Well, I quick-hopped into the hall to grab a fire extinguisher and ran smack into two dignified old English biddies. I was barefoot, just wearing my shorts, no shirt on—and they let out a yell and reported to the manager that a naked wildman was running amok in the hallway. That's when we were asked to leave the Savoy."

By the time *War Lover* was completed Steve had signed for another war film in the States. In *Hell is for Heroes* he etched the role of a cold-eyed, gun-happy killer who revels in trench fighting, makes friends with nobody and is finally killed by the enemy. The script was brutal and bitter, and McQueen's downbeat role did little to advance his career, despite the fact that *Heroes* was ultimately more successful at the box office than *War Lover*.

McQueen was soon savoring the joys of rough-country cycle riding. ("I first tried dirt riding on a bike I'd borrowed from a neighbor, and the sense of being out there on your own was tremendous. No preparation. Just kick it over, drive up the side of a hill—and you're free!")

In March, 1962, he entered the Open Novice class for a California cycle event dubbed the Four Aces Moose Run. He took a third in this race but had his problems.

"For one thing, they wouldn't let me get my wheel into the line at the start," he claimed. "These people didn't think much of an actor. They didn't trust me then, just wouldn't move over for me. But I got a trophy out of it, plus a set of blistered hands."

McQueen later talked about this aspect of cycle racing: "All that jumpin' and crashin' around over the countryside can tear your hands up pretty bad. You're tense at the beginning, and you grip the bars too hard. Later you get more experience and you learn to relax. After a lot of riding your hands get calloused. But that takes time."

Steve was learning his dirt-cycle technique from Bud Ekins and Don Mitchell, veterans whose many trophies testified to their knowledge of rough-country competition.

In that same month (March of '62) Steve got an opportunity to compete at Sebring (along with Stirling Moss) as a member of the BMC team under John Cooper.

"I drove two cars that weekend in Florida," he said. "They had a kind of warm-up race there on Saturday, a three-hour production go in which all of us BMC drivers were put into Austin-Healey Sprites. I finished ninth in a field of two-dozen-plus. Moss was third—and I know that Pedro Rodriguez and Innes Ireland were also in the race, but I don't recall where they finished. The next day, in the big twelve-hour Sebring main event, I drove a Le Mans Special for Cooper."

This car was a special-bodied racing Healey Sprite, much faster than the production models, which had won the Index of Performance at Le Mans. Steve's co-driver was John Colgate (of the toothpaste Colgates).

"I had a close call in the Esses," admitted McQueen. "I'd been battling with another car for the better part of an hour and we were both going all-out on this particular lap. I was getting ready to gear down for the Esses and was doing over a hundred in fourth. When I grabbed the shift knob to bring it down to third the darn thing popped right off in my hand. Fifty feet of sliding, and I was able to get things under control again."

That mishap resulted in a corrected design fault. The rubber threads on the shift knobs in all production Sprites were replaced with steel threads: Demonstrating that racing *does* improve the breed—if the drivers survive.

After seven hours, the McQueen/Colgate Healey was leading its class. Their run was shaping toward a trophy when the car began spitting smoke from its exhaust. Colgate was at the wheel as the Sprite rolled to a sad halt; a defect in the casing had caused an oil loss. The overheated engine had thrown a rod.

Designer Donald Healey was most impressed with Steve: "McQueen's performance was exceptional. He'll go somewhere as a driver if he can find the time to do it."

A month after Sebring (having taken delivery of his Formula Jr. Cooper from England) McQueen swept the field at Del Mar, winning both days. Steve took the car to Cotati and clocked fast time through the traps before engine trouble waylaid him. He worked all night on the engine, preparing it for Sunday's main. These efforts seemed to be paying off in the early laps, as he battled driver Ed Leslie for the lead.

"We were into a real ding-dong for first," declared

Steve. "Then water began leaking into the combustion chamber from a split in the head. Due to this, I lost power in a spark plug, which put me on three cylinders. Naturally, I dropped behind Leslie. This bugged me, so I began pushing harder than I should have, taking the turns at full opposite lock, sliding into the dirt and grass. . . . I finally got too far out of shape and clipped one of those little circuit loudspeakers they have near the road's edge, just wiped it right out. Then I caught a rock in my goggles, which all but blinded me, and I sailed off into the weeds."

Neile had been spectating at the race and saw Steve shoot off course. She was furious at him for deliberately exceeding his limits and began telling him so in front of the crowd. ("She was speaking for a lot of racers' wives, so I shut up and let her bawl me out. I figured I had it coming.")

"I never got used to his racing," admitted Neile. "It was a world of Steve's I could never really enter."

A week later, running the repaired open-cockpit Cooper at Santa Barbara, Steve won both of his events, in addition to driving a borrowed MG-B in a production race. ("I was leading until I ran out of gas!")

When Steve returned home after the weekend in Santa Barbara he found a grim-faced lawyer sitting on his doorstep. The man had a restraining order.

"The film studio had decided that I would either stop racing or stop making pictures. They gave me twenty-four hours to make up my mind. Which upset me, angered me. I took most of those twenty-four hours thinking about whether I wanted to go on racing, earning my money on the track, or whether I wanted to continue being an actor on the studio's terms. It was a very tough decision for me to reach. Still, I had Neile and our two young children to consider, and that made the difference. I signed their paper."

McQueen's decision was a wise one, since his biggest

picture was on the immediate horizon. Had he retired from acting at this juncture he would have missed being in *The Great Escape*.

On May 30 he left the States for Munich, Germany, to join the cast. This production was based on the factual story of the escape of seventy-six RAF prisoners from a German prison compound during World War II and was to be filmed by John Sturges, who had directed *The Magnificent Seven* in Mexico. Sturges had picked McQueen to play a cocky American prisoner nicknamed the Cooler King because of his frequent solitary confinement as a rule-breaker. For his co-starring services Steve would be paid $100,000 and allowed to stunt-ride a cycle.

"John and I worked a hairy motorcycle chase into the script," said McQueen. "The idea was this Cooler King character makes good his escape by stealing a cycle, gets chased cross-country by German cyclists and loses them by jumping this big barbed wire fence with his bike."

By inserting this cycle sequence into *The Great Escape*, Steve had out-foxed the studio; now the executives had no choice. Steve *would* race. On film, and at *their* risk.

Interiors for the picture were shot at the Bavaria studios in Munich, while all of the outdoor location shooting was done at a specially constructed camp (simulating a German prison compound) built by technicians just outside the city. Two of the individuals who would later function in key posts in McQueen's own production company were directly associated with *The Great Escape*: Robert Relyea handled a variety of duties for Sturges (even stunt-crashing a plane when no one else was available to do it), while Jack Reddish (who'd sold Steve his Lotus back in California) was first assistant director.

"And Bud Ekins went along as a stunt rider," said Steve. "We had four bikes for this film. I was running a TT

Special forty-cubic-inch 650 Triumph. We painted it olive drab and put on a luggage rack and an old seat to make it look like a wartime BMW. We couldn't really use a BMW, not at the speeds we were running, since those old babies were rigid-frame jobs. They wouldn't stand the punishment."

The local reaction to McQueen, Ekins and the other riders amused Steve. "The first time we tried out the bikes at full chat the Bavarians just gaped, open-mouthed. They didn't believe that a bike could *go* that fast over this kind of uphill-downhill terrain."

In the filmed chase Steve blasts over the Rhine countryside, hotly pursued by Nazi cyclists. McQueen enjoyed this type of action so much that he doubled for his pursuers, wearing a German helmet and uniform, with Ekins bouncing along beside him in the sidecar. ("They intercut these scenes—and there I am on the screen, me chasing me!")

The one stunt in the picture Steve *didn't* do involved a sixty-foot cycle jump over a high barbed wire fence. Steve attempted it and failed, and Bud Ekins did the actual jump on film.

"I always felt a little guilty about that," confessed Steve. "A lot of people thought it was me making that jump, but I've never tried to hide the truth about it. I could handle the jump *now*, I'm sure. Back in sixty-two I just didn't quite have the savvy."

There were delays in the production. Things went wrong on the set; the weather caused shutdowns. All of which caused Steve to become restless. He talked the producer into providing him with a 300-SL Mercedes sports sedan.

"I told him it was my therapy," he said. "Told him I had to have some kind of decent machine or I'd flip out. So I got it. Next night I woke Neile up and told her I was taking off for a run and that I'd be back late the next night. I climbed into the SL and drove out of Munich across the woodland into the mountains and on down through the Brenner Pass toward Italy."

As Steve rolled along the curving road a pair of full-race Ferraris, with competition numbers painted on them, boomed up on him. ("They were out practicing for a race, so I decided to give them some practice, have a go with 'em. I got on it and we had a real ding-dong all the way down.")

By the time they'd reached the floor of the pass Steve had burned out the brakes on the Mercedes, and his car bore the scars of a few stone road markers and fence posts he'd side-swiped enroute.

"I barely managed to hang close to them," Steve admitted. "Compared to a competition Ferrari the SL handled like a tub of water. Anyhow, when we reached the border the guy in the lead Ferrari was very happy. He didn't know who I was, but he evidently thought it had been a bloody good motor race, especially since he beat me. He insisted on buying me some wine—and then I insisted on buying *him* some wine and I got drunk and he took me to his house to sober up. I was back in Munich the next night, ready to go on the set the following morning. I'd worked out all the kinks with that SL."

When *The Great Escape* was released in 1963 Steve's full screen potential was finally realized; public and critics alike were mightily impressed with his gutsy performance, and the film was solid gold at the box office.

McQueen completed his next film, *Love With the Proper Stranger*, in New York with Natalie Wood as his co-star, a drama which cast him as a musician (a horn player) involved with a troubled girl. *Newsweek* termed his work "brilliant indeed," adding that McQueen had now achieved his breakthrough as a major film star, doing it "his way, on his terms." They quoted him as admitting he was difficult: "Yeah, I am. I buck the system. Guys who have been through a lot of hassles are going to hold out for what's right, for the truth. I've formed my own company, Solar Productions, to get some control, some creative leverage in what I do."

And he was back into racing again.

The day after the wrap-up scene on *Stranger* Steve flew back to California in time to enter a top cycle event, the 1963 running of the Greenhorn Enduro across the Mojave. The Greenhorn had been staged once a year since the mid-1940's and attracted the toughest riders mounted on machines built to take a beating. The run was 500 miles over a wheel-bending, back-snapping course laid out across the southern Mojave Desert. The competitors ran over old and new trails, dirt roads, through old mining towns, up rugged slopes studded with boulders and thorny cactus, along seemingly endless stretches of dry, desolate country, on through the El Paso mountains and valleys into the Rand Range of hills, over a raw land heavily potholed with abandoned mine shafts dating back to gold-rush days. It involved an overnight stop, during which the riders slept as their pit crews replaced nuts and bolts, changed tires, cleaned jammed air filters and tightened spokes on the badly battered cycles.

More than 7,000 pounds of lime were used to mark the course every year, and each run varied. Only one element remained constant: the savage toughness of 500 miles of sun and sand.

McQueen had never run so fierce a race. "My hands went," he said. "They were hamburger meat, fighting the bike bars the way I had to do. You're doing maybe seventy, really honkin' on, and you see a big ditch comin' at you. Well, you tense up and grab those bars and try to hang tight. You'll hit holes that'll bend the bars right down."

Steve survived the first day's run, sliding and slipping and gunning his cycle along the route, but just twenty miles from the finish he blew a cylinder. ("I pulled the plug and limped the rest of the way in on one cylinder.")

Competing out of District 37 within the jurisdiction of the American Motorcycle Association, the most competitive district in the United States for beginning riders, McQueen won enough points to move up to amateur status (from novice) in just one year. A bike veteran commented on this: "Out of some five thousand new riders every year only about five hundred move up in class that fast. Steve was outstanding, no question of that."

John Huetter, editor of *Dirt Bike*, recalled one of Steve's races at Red Rock Canyon. "No more than one hundred yards from the start McQueen's bike struck a rock and the right pedal was sheared off. Which meant he couldn't do any of the rough sections standing up, or, as we say, 'riding the pegs.' Yet he went on to finish in the top ten on one peg. Which was incredible."

McQueen earned his spurs in bike racing by "showing them how thick my mud is." He had to work doubly hard to overcome the image of the "soft movie star." Perhaps this is why he pushed himself beyond the safety point again and again. He took a lot of spills to prove he had the nerve and courage to stick with the fastest riders.

"These guys are tough cookies," said McQueen. "They've learned to survive, and they have a strict code. You don't lie about the sport. And you don't cheat at it. You play it straight. I broke a shoulder and I broke an arm in two places *and* I had four stitches in my head, all before these people accepted me for real. I paid my dues and I was accepted. They knew I wasn't out there for publicity or for laughs; I was out there to run."

Steve ran a San Gabriel Hare and Hounds event that season, earning a class second. He explained this particular form of bike racing: "In Hare and Hounds one or two guys set out ahead of the pack, laying out the course by dropping bags of lime along the way. They usually pick the roughest kind of terrain to lead you through, and you never know quite what to expect or what's ahead. You're running flat out with all the other hounds, maybe five hundred guys, chasing the hare. That's how you learn to 'read' terrain."

McQueen's financial status improved as fast as his racing status, and he was soon shopping with Neile for a new home. The old one on Nichols Canyon no longer suited the family.

The real estate agent finally located what she termed "the ideal place." McQueen was dubious; she hadn't mentioned a price.

"We drove through this electric gate," related Steve, "and started swinging around this mountain with a rock wall on one side and all these trees. . . . Then we came to the top, under a big stone archway into this medieval Spanish courtyard—and my eyes are popping. I said to Neile, 'Don't ask the price. We can't afford this layout.' But the real estate lady took us inside and that was that. We bought it."

The price was "over $250,000" and it was quite a step forward from the cold-water walk-up in Greenwich Village. The two-story mansion was a combination of ranch-style, Mediterranean and modern, sitting high atop Oakmont Drive in Brentwood, with a clear view of the Pacific. Among the special features: a marble fireplace, an Olympic-sized swimming pool, a den the size of a tennis court, an outdoor playhouse for the children, a custom pool table in the sunken living room.

In recognition of their new status, Neile gifted Steve with a fabulous new car, a three-liter Berlinetta Lusso Ferrari with fifteen-inch Borrani wire wheels. This twelve-cylinder beauty became the prize item in McQueen's racing stable, which now included his XK-SS Jag, a Mini-Cooper S, a sports Cobra, the British Land Rover, a Lincoln town car, his Triumph Bonneville, a street Honda—and an exotic assortment of borrowed dirt bikes from Bud Ekins' motorcycle shop. This collection of high-powered machinery spilled out of his garage onto the vast cobbled motor court of his new home, and Steve continued to add to it whenever a special car or bike caught his eye.

Proof that he'd truly "arrived" as a public personality came with his appearance on the cover of *Life* (riding a cycle with Neile behind him) in mid-July, 1963. The inside story described him as filmdom's "hottest new star" and went on to report that "he talks the lingo of the rough world that spawned him—a world of hipsters, racing drivers, beach boys, drifters and carnival barkers. McQueen has been all of these."

Indeed, Steve had not turned his back on this "rough world" of his past, and now that he was financially strong he determined to aid the problem boys at Chino. He set up an annual scholarship fund for "best student" at the Boys Republic and began visiting the school on a regular basis, talking "the real goods" to the young men there.

"They really appreciate seeing him," said one of the counselors at Chino. "They listen to him, relate to him. He doesn't preach to them. He broke the mold and they figure they can break it too."

In recognition of his newly won stardom, when McQueen went to Paramount to star in *Soldier in the Rain* with Jackie Gleason he was assigned the dressing room once occupied by Gary Cooper. Steve had personally chosen this film property and was tied into the production via his company; it was to be the first of many films to involve Solar Productions.

One of the scenes called for him to wrestle a stunt man through a latticework partition in a savagely staged bar brawl. In the melee Steve was smashed flat across a pool table.

"That stunt guy knocked me dingy for a while," he admitted. "Still, I'd rather do this kind of action scene than the heavy emotional stuff. You have to reach inside yourself for the heavy scenes and it's not an easy thing to do. You have to turn yourself inside out, empty all of your emotional pockets. That always puts me uptight."

Workouts at the studio gym between sequences helped ease his tension. He punched bags, hefted 130-pound weights, and did sit-ups on a tilt board to toughen his stomach muscles.

In *Soldier in the Rain* he tackled the role of a comic-type Army sidekick to Gleason. Since there were several golfing bits in the picture, Steve modified the motorized golf cart Paramount provided, gleefully bragging to Gleason (who hated speed), "Man, I bet this is the last time you'll ever see a golf cart burn rubber!"

After the final scene had been shot Gleason solemnly presented McQueen with a pair of Saint Christopher cufflinks, informing him that they should be worn to protect him in his speed jaunts. ("I didn't tell Jackie, but you just *don't* wear cufflinks in a bike race!")

5

RACING AGAINST THE BEST

The small, sleepy town of Bay City, Texas, woke up one day in January, 1964, to find itself starring in a movie. Director Robert Mulligan had moved his cast into Bay City for location work in the film version of Horton Foote's Broadway play *The Traveling Lady*. (The final release title, based on a song in the film, was *Baby, the Rain Must Fall*.)

In this downbeat drama, Steve McQueen etched the role of a problem-ridden guitarist/singer, an ex-convict named Henry Thomas who cannot make the transitional adjustment to a wife and child. Actress Lee Remick was playing McQueen's wife. Their outdoor location scenes in Texas took a full month to complete.

Again, as in his last film, Steve was injured in a realistic bar fight, described by one set witness as "a savage knockdown, in which tables, chairs and pitchers of beer were sent flying . . . McQueen was wild . . . he'll try anything."

The director, applying an ice pack to Steve's cut eye, added his personal estimation of the actor's drive. "He's not afraid to *use* himself when he acts. Steve has what I call a kind of daring theatricality."

"Heck, what I've got is a black eye!" grinned McQueen.

Bodily injury, on or off a film set, has never slowed Steve down. He described one desert cycle race, typical of many: "I did an end-over-end at seventy and was all wrapped up in the bike. I didn't know my arm was busted. I got back on, with about forty more miles to go, and noticed that I couldn't shift, but I finished anyhow, taking a third in my class. Then they looked at my arm and, sure enough, it was broken."

Such accidents panic his studio, but Steve shrugs them aside. Asked by a sports reporter to list his racing mishaps, he admitted to an incredible series of physical injuries: "I've broken my arm in two places, my foot in six. Then I've broken a shoulder bone, knocked out some teeth, had plastic surgery on my face, had my head split open more than once and my nose busted at least three times, snapped a couple of ribs, smashed up my knuckles, broke all the toes on one foot . . . and I don't remember what else. If you race cycles, you take spills. You're out there twisting the tiger's tail. Man, I've been thrown into the air so often I can peg the soft landing spots. I just kind of wiggle my rear end in the right direction and head for one!"

Steve blandly recounted a "double-race afternoon" at Hi Vista when he competed for the Pacific West Coast Championship Scrambles crown: "There was this big pile-up in the fourth lap, and to avoid the tangle I hit a tree, split my mouth open and knocked some teeth loose. But I was okay. I won the race. Then I entered the second go that same afternoon, ran the event with my face all puffed and bandaged, and won that one too. My only worry that night was how Neile would react when I came home looking like I did. But she was cool about it; Neile is used to this kind of thing."

McQueen won five cycle trophies in 1964, all in scrambles.

Scrambling was invented by the British, the point being to compete over the roughest possible terrain. One of these early British riders coined a name for the event when he dubbed it "a rare old scramble." The sport developed overseas in the postwar years, then moved to the States when trail bikes began to become popular in the late 1950's and early '60's.

Hare Scrambling, in which McQueen excels, is quite similar to Hare and Hounds: A long line of riders form at the start, behind a restraining rope, with entrants often numbering in the hundreds. In progressive waves, based on engine displacement, the riders are sent off in great clouds of dust and exhaust across a brutal stretch of desert to the course itself—which is usually two to five miles distant. Then they begin to circle this course (which often measures out to a twenty-mile loop) for a set number of bone-cracking laps, stopping at checkpoints to pick up colored markers which prove that each rider has followed the full route.

Actually, Hare Scrambles, as one veteran observer describes it, "is a real torture test for riders, combining the most intimidating features of the classic Hare and Hounds with the sheer speed and danger of a closed-course scrambles race. Riders find themselves lured, for example, over the rim of a deep arroyo at impossible speed, as well as across stretches of closed-spaced ditch jumps (thank-you-mams) made particularly interesting by sharp rocks and thickets of spiny cholla cactus. Machines and riders take a real beating; each race has its assorted lacerations and broken bones, and the competitors who can manage the full route without easing their pace have to be in excellent physical condition. Bodies take a tremendous pounding. Perhaps it is one way to find out just how much honest animal is left under the civilized veneer we all wear."

For that trophy-winning '64 season in California, McQueen competed on a modified Triumph, race-prepared by his friend Bud Ekins (out of Ekins' shop in Sherman Oaks). This Triumph Bonneville desert bike featured high pipes, braced foot pegs and a special skid plate to protect the underside of the engine in rocky country. The compression had been lowered (for reliability) on the basically stock Bonneville engine and the cycle was fitted with twin Amal carbs and paper-pack air cleaners (to filter out sand and dust). All in all, a neat machine—and fast.

"Bud is one of the top bike racers in the game," McQueen declared. "He's also a serious businessman. People tend to think of cyclists as leather-jacket nuts. Sure, we wear leather when we ride, because that desert can rip you up bad if you take a spill in ordinary street clothes. But we're just people under the leather, not freaks—doctors, attorneys, mechanics. . . . We usually take our families along on these weekend cycle runs. Bud's family and mine are very close; we all get along fine together. We stuff everybody into a pickup, tie down the bikes in back, and take off for the high desert."

McQueen is not a man naturally given to poetic expression, but when he talks about the desert the poetic flavor is evident: "I tell you, there's nothin' like the sweet smell of puckerbushes and cactus and warm sand out there in that desert. . . . The kids play in the dunes and the wives root for their men or talk fashions. You come back from a race, all sweaty, mud-and-grease covered—and here are the ladies, like a bunch of bright flowers, sitting on the sand, talking about the latest style in slacks and blouses. See, we're not Hell's Angels. We're just plain family people out there having a go."

Steve found himself in local Los Angeles headlines three times that summer: in May, when he caught a prowler on his Brentwood property and held the man captive with a 9-mm Mauser until police arrived; in July, when he appeared before the L.A. City Council speaking as a concerned citizen with regard to keeping the land in the Santa Monica mountains free from commercial interests; and in August, when he was photographed in Beverly Hills, happily dancing the Watusi with the President's daughter, Luci Johnson.

By September he was back into cycle competition and in the major league. (Luckily for McQueen, his studio bosses never put up any serious objections to his cycle competition, since they considered it far less dangerous than auto racing.) This time Steve was set to run in Europe against the world's best two-wheelers. He'd been accepted as part of the five-man American cycle team for the International Six-Day Trials in East Germany, the year's peak prestige event for professional rough riders. The other four Americans competing with Steve that September were John Steen, Cliff Coleman, Bud Ekins and his brother Dave.

In just two and a half years of dirt riding McQueen had acquired enough skill and cycle savvy to qualify him for this top pro event. His days as novice and amateur were over; he was now running against the best from England, East Germany, Sweden, Holland, Spain, Russia, Czechoslovakia, Poland, Finland, Scotland and Austria.

It was agreed that Neile would remain in California with their children until the race was over, then join Steve in Frankfort. McQueen took off for London, where the team picked up their racing equipment (500- and 650-cc Triumphs) from the factory in Coventry. ("My bike was a 650-cc forty-cubic-inch job running knobby tires with a few extra goodies installed.")

The five Americans met the British team (who ranked as

prime competition) and a quick friendship developed among the riders. ("They gave us the special tubes and chains that we needed and filled us in on a lot of data on the race, inside stuff we appreciated knowing.")

The International Six-Days Trial began in Britain in 1913, with 170 riders off the line for that first event. It had grown each year until, by this race in 1964, there were 226 entrants set to run more than 1,200 miles (in 200-mile daily stages) through woods, up mountains, along rock-strewn trails and cart paths—fighting time as well as terrain.

As one participant outlined the rules: "Once underway, each rider has to maintain an average which depends on engine capacity. The rider follows arrows which mark out the course, getting his route card stamped along the way to prove that he has not taken a short cut. Keeping an eye on the clock and his mileage-counter, he must adjust his speed to hit the time clock on the right minute. His time through each section is stamped on a card, and if he loses too many points for being late into a check area his record is spoiled and his medal is gone."

The immediate goal for each man was a gold medal, awarded to the rider who could finish the entire run with no marks lost on time. (Silver and bronze medals were also awarded to those losing only minimal points along the route.) The *ultimate* goal, for the winning team, was the privilege of hosting the following year's race in its home country. ("We wanted to bring it here, to the U.S.A., right out to the desert.") East Germany, whose team had won the trial in 1963, was current host.

In England the Americans obtained a van, had an American flag painted on the side, loaded in their racing bikes and tools, and headed for Germany.

"It was a long trip," said McQueen, "and we spelled each other at the wheel. We drove all night, then got hung up for four hours at the border. We never quite understood the long delay, but it seemed to have something to do with their interest in Western money. Anyhow, we finally made it across to Erfurt and into our dormitories. It was kind of weird, being there behind the Iron Curtain, with everybody watching us.

"I remember the night before the race they had a parade of nations in this big hall, about the size of a football stadium, and the guys from each team marched for their country. I stood up there, holding the American flag, right between the Russians and the East Germans, and it was an emotional moment for me. I was really proud to be there."

Steve revealed a humorous sidelight to racing in alien territory: "For breakfast, in the mess hall, they gave each of us a strip of cold eel, some awful kind of gelatine, a piece of green tomato and a cup of coffee black enough to dye your socks in. We asked if this stuff was the usual breakfast and they said no, that this is what the Russian scientists decided we should eat to be at maximum health for the race. Cold eel for breakfast. Wow!"

Each of the 226 competing cycles was officially scrutinized, with vital parts marked and stamped to prevent an exchange of machinery. The rules required each rider to repair his machine from parts and tools carried enroute. No swaps or exchanges of new outside parts were permitted. At the end of each day's run all riders had to return their mounts to the official paddock where they were locked up, with no overnight repairs allowed.

Here, in ranked rows, were the Czech team's CZ 250's, the Russian Jawas, the sensational MZ machines of East Germany, BSA's from Britain, the Husqvarnas of Sweden, the KTM's of Austria and the American team Triumphs.

Each rider was assigned a competition number which was firmly affixed to his machine; Steve's was 278. On the starting line in East Germany, wearing his striped crash helmet, black leather jacket and heavy-duty boots, gloved hands poised on the throttle, racing goggles masking his eyes, Terrence Steven McQueen was a long way from the glamor and comfort of a Hollywood sound stage. There would be no favored attention given him here; he was simply one rider in a vast field, set to run against his racing peers.

Which was exactly how he wanted it. He had fought hard to get here.

The sky was dark with rain when the first cycles exploded away from the line. Engine size determined starting positions, with the smaller 250-cc machines released ahead of the larger 500- and 650-cc types—which meant that the muddy course was chopped and dangerous by the time McQueen was flagged off in his 650 Triumph. ("Worse yet, I'd never raced in the wet!")

John Steen was the first American to get into trouble. On that initial day's run Steen dropped thirteen points due to having lost his way, which meant he could not possibly win a gold medal. However, the other four Americans did very well, indeed, scoring in sixth position as a team by the end of the first day. By the close of the second day they continued brilliantly, ending the section in a tied lead with the British team.

McQueen recorded his memories of the event in graphic detail: "We were in first position, with England, and were actually leading overall on bonus points. At this stage I was definitely lined up for a gold medal and going hard. Part of the last run of this second day was over an open road cutting through a forest. I was dicing with the British champ, John Gills, a marvelous racer, and we were moving along at full chat in the rain.

"We could figure where the highway would bend by watching the way the trees lined up. But we got fooled, because at one point the trees marched straight ahead while the road turned. We came into this turn, a full turkey leg, at about eighty—and began sliding for traction. I went off the road and down into a cart track, taking a fall. I saw marks where other riders had got themselves into the same kind of trouble. My cheek was cut from the goggles but nothing was broken, so I picked the twigs and leaves out of my ears and looked around for my bike. The tail pipe was smashed. I groaned, flipped a tool out of my back pocket, and bent the pipe back into usable shape.

"I was in a sweat because if you're three minutes late into a checkpoint you lose your chance for a gold medal. I decided I'd played it dumb by braking hard in the mud and dumping. But I made it to the next checkpoint in time, and there was no problem. I was still in the running."

On the third day the image of a team victory dissolved as Bud Ekins clipped a stone bridge at speed and broke his leg. And by dusk of this same day, with the relentless rain still miring the roads and pounding the circuit into shifting mud, McQueen's luck ran out.

"Up until then things looked good for me. I was getting the hang of racing in the wet, getting relaxed about it, and the bike was perking along. Then I busted a chain on a steep hill climb. I rolled through the timing point, repaired the chain, and within a half mile another link snapped. After I'd fixed the chain again I was running four to five minutes late, meaning my gold medal was gone for sure if I didn't make up the lost time by the next checkpoint."

Steve kept increasing his speed, blasting the powerful 650 Triumph through the rain-gray German countryside, mud and rocks spraying back from his sliding wheels; he was "riding the edge," using all of his skill to regain those lost minutes.

And he *was* gaining them back, minute by minute. . . .

Whipping over the brow of a slope lined with spectators and out along the narrow lip of a pine-thick ravine, McQueen was not prepared for the abrupt emergency directly ahead of him.

"Out of nowhere, this spectator on a bike cut right across the course. He didn't hear me or see me, he just blundered out into my path. When he looked up and saw me bearing down on him he hit the panic button. I was planning to squeak by him on the left and was cranking it on, figuring he'd leave me room to get past. But when he panicked he cut left at the last split-second and shut the door on me.

"Now there was this thick crowd of people. I didn't want to hurt anyone, not the guy on the other bike or any of the spectators, so I put my Triumph over the side of the ravine, buzzed off into space and unloaded in midair. My bike sailed about eight feet over my head and cut down some small pine trees, while I bounced a few times, ending up against a rock. My face was gashed, my kneecaps were torn up and I had some nice red tool marks on my rear end, but I'd survived.

"My bike hadn't. I took off the front fender. The wheel was badly dented and the tire was shot. Which might have been all right, but the forks were bent clear back to the chassis. I managed to ride back to our van, but my run was over. That spill had cost me more than a medal, it cost me the bloody race."

The remaining three Americans finished the full six days. Dave Ekins and Cliff Coleman won gold medals and John Steen took home a silver medal.

"We were a battered-looking lot," summed up McQueen. "Bud's leg was busted. Steen had five stitches in his chin from a crack-up. Dave was all black-and-blue from having unloaded on pavement doing about eighty. And I was a mess. But we'd left some scratch marks over there; we'd gone against the best of Europe and our team had come away with three medals for the U.S. And even though I was disappointed in not finishing, the experience of competing in the sixty-four trial was one of the high points of my life."

6

TROUBLE IN THE ORIENT

Two days after the cycle race in East Germany Neile met Steve at the Frankfort airport. The children were home; this would be their time together. They spent the weekend touring the historic German city, then took the train into Paris, where they rented the penthouse at the Crillon.

"People were wonderful to us in Paris," said Neile. "The French are diehard movie buffs and Steve was so well known he couldn't get a foot down the street before being swamped by fans. He had to wear glasses and a false mustache and beard when we went out to dinner! We attended the opening of one of his films, and I posed for the cover of *Elle*, the fashion magazine, wearing a Lanvin gown. We were all over the place!"

Beyond Paris, they drove through France and Spain, from Barcelona to Majorca, then into Belgium, taking any side road that looked promising, lunching at small inns, enjoying the peace and solitude. "We got lost for a while," declared Neile. "But it was good to be lost, good to be free and alone, just the two of us. We needed that time together."

Steve was due back in Hollywood in January to film interiors for *The Cincinnati Kid*. This offbeat movie pitted him against sharkish Edward G. Robinson. As a card-clever challenger, McQueen battled Robinson, the old poker veteran, for the title of "The Man." Much of the action was set in New Orleans, and Steve saw to it that the script included at least one fast-action sequence, wherein the Kid is trapped by toughs and must fight his way clear by smashing through a window. Essentially, however, the film was a tense character study, a clash of giants, youth against age—and Steve's role was somewhat restrictive in a physical sense. Yet his card skills, polished in the service and in New York, helped him deliver a solid performance.

During those early months of 1965 Steve's mind was once again on cars, not cards. He and director John Sturges (who was also a speed buff, driving a fast Porsche and serving as his son's go-kart pit crew) had pooled their talents on a new film property, *Day of the Champion*, referred to as "the inside story of professional motor racing." The plot concerned a crash-prone Formula 1 Grand Prix driver who becomes world champion "despite severe psychological problems." The theme was that of a man against his own limits in a sport requiring a human being to put his life on the line each time he races.

The film was to be shot in Europe during the 1966 Grand Prix season, and McQueen (insured for two million dollars) was to star. Warners agreed to finance the film, but not until McQueen and Sturges had sunk $25,000 into preproduction costs, part of which involved mounting a camera on a full-race machine in order to obtain dramatic high-speed race footage at Riverside. ("We had to *show*

Warners just how exciting this one could be.")

With a script by award-winner Edward Anhalt, Sturges and McQueen left for Europe that summer (after Steve had completed *The Cincinnati Kid*) to scout drivers and locations. Stirling Moss (now retired after a near-fatal crash in 1962) was to be production consultant, and he joined them overseas at the end of May for the Grand Prix of Monaco.

This race, through the narrow streets of Monte Carlo, was a thriller, with one car losing a wheel and slamming a stack of hay bales and another flipping off the circuit into the bay. (Frogmen had to rescue the driver.) Steve was impressed with ex-cycle champ John Surtees, who brought his Ferrari into fourth, and by the Scottish BRM team driver Jackie Stewart, who was third. McQueen signed both of them for *Champion*, and found out, from Stewart, that he (Steve) had ancestors in Scotland. ("He told me they have several McQueen castles over there!")

Steve also spectated at the French Grand Prix in June and at the German Grand Prix in August, arranging exclusive contracts to film both events the following season as part of *Day of the Champion.*

McQueen was actually competing with director John Frankenheimer for 1966 European race sites. Backed by MGM, Frankenheimer was preparing his own full-scale Formula 1 film, *Grand Prix*, to star a pal of Steve's, James Garner. Eight million dollars of MGM's money was committed to this Cinerama production. Both films had American driver/heroes who became world champions in Formula 1 competition, and the rivalry was intense.

"We wanted to beat MGM to the punch," said one of McQueen's crew. "But Frankenheimer had a head start, and Steve still had two films to make before he could do *Champion.*"

McQueen had signed for *Nevada Smith*, with location work in the South, plus *The Sand Pebbles*, scheduled for shooting in the Orient. However, since his racing film was not due to roll until the beginning of the '66 season in Europe, Steve felt he could pull it off and make all three films, back to back.

While automotive writer Ken Purdy labored on a revision of Anhalt's screenplay, Steve headed for location on *Nevada Smith,* his first Western since *The Magnificent Seven.* He was cast as the bitterly determined young halfbreed who rides in blood pursuit of the white men who murdered his parents. This part called for a variety of physical action with fist, gun and knife. In the course of the film Steve is captured and sent into the swamps as a chain-gang prisoner. He escapes to seek his final vengeance. It was a rugged, demanding role, and few actors were as qualified.

The scenic backgrounds were spectacular and authentic; the action began at Mammoth, near Banner Peak and Mount Ritter. Neile flew up to be with Steve for part of the shooting but soon had to return to their children in California.

"Steve didn't like to see her leave," reported a set worker. "Her being there kept him at an even temper. A man can get kinda loco in the high country!"

Three weeks later the cast was moved to Baton Rouge for a series of day-and-night sequences in the wilderness bayous of the Atchafalaya Basin (and at the prison compound at Fort Vincent). Alone and under pressure in his exhausting role, McQueen phoned Neile and demanded that she join him on location. She said no, that she had to remain with the children. Bring them along, he told her. No, not to such a dangerous area.

Neile recalled their argument: "Whenever we're away from each other for any period of time we fight like mad on the phone. We have real marathons. Neither of us wants to hang up until the argument is settled—and, as a result, our phone bills are ridiculous. Well, this time Steve was

71

nervous, tense, really uptight, wading through dirty water, coping with leeches, spiders and swamp snakes. He was plainly miserable and in an awful temper. Why in the world wasn't I up there with him? Why should I be living in luxury in Brentwood having tea with my girlfriends while he fought those crazy swamps? I gave in and told him I was packing that night."

Thus, Neile was on the set (a longboat) when Steve waded up to his armpits in the slime of Two O'Clock Bayou. But he was smiling. His old lady was with him, which made it okay.

"We're a real unit," he told a reporter. "I just don't function when my old lady's not around. She digs me, understands my moods, keeps me in balance. She even brings me Mexican beer. And she's sexier than any movie starlet! Man, we *need* each other!"

The day after the McQueens returned to Hollywood from Baton Rouge (having completed the final scenes on *Nevada Smith*) an alarming phone call sent them hurrying to San Francisco: Steve's mother was critically ill at the Mount Zion Hospital. A friend had passed along the message: Hurry, the doctor's afraid she's dying. Of a brain hemorrhage.

McQueen found his mother in a coma—and sent Neile to a hotel. "I'll wait here. I'm sure she'll come out of this. I feel so darned strong; maybe I can give her some of my strength."

But he couldn't. The coma deepened, and Julian Crawford McQueen Berri died without regaining consciousness. At fifty-five her life ended peacefully.

After the funeral in Los Angeles, at Forest Lawn, her friends told Steve how much pleasure his mother had gotten out of the Volkswagen he'd bought for her, how happy she'd been in the final months of her life, tooling the perky little VW up and down the hills of San Francisco. She'd even been planning a new start—opening a one-woman travel agency. Her four-room apartment, located close to Fisherman's Wharf in the North Beach area, had been furnished with zest and flair. Scattered through it were photos of Steve and Neile and of her two grandchildren, as well as numerous movie fan magazines featuring write-ups on her son's career. ("She saw all of your films at least twice," Steve was told.)

Hearing all this, McQueen lowered his head. "I guess she loved me more than I loved her," he admitted. "I tried, but. . . ."

Reporters swarmed in. He waved them away. "No interviews. This is private. No comment."

From that day forward Steve never made another public statement regarding his mother; he closed and locked that particular room in his past.

Just a month after his mother's death McQueen made final plans for their location trip to the Orient on *The Sand Pebbles*. A problem had arisen: Neile received a firm studio offer to co-star with Marlon Brando in his next film. She had been talking to Steve about resuming her career and he had told her he wouldn't object. This new offer could mean a major break for Neile.

But she said no. She and the children would go with Steve to Taiwan. He needed her. The tension caused by their brief separation on *Nevada Smith* told her that. Brando could find another co-star; she didn't want to look for another husband.

"There was never any question about our going with Steve," she later declared. "We didn't want to leave him alone for months in a foreign country. I decided that one film star in the family was enough."

Two square miles of Taiwan's Keelung Harbor had been carefully rebuilt by studio technicians to pass for Shanghai as it looked in the 1920's. The studio had also put $250,000 into building a replica of the *San Pablo*, a fully functioning, 150-foot steel-hulled '20's gunboat, complete

73

with an antique steam engine weighing in at 41,280 pounds. (Due to such painstaking attention to period details, plus star salaries and delays caused by bad weather, the original budget of eight million would total out to twelve million, making it, in Hollywood terms, a "blockbuster.")

The picture's background was authentic, involving young revolutionaries who in 1926 forged a Chinese Republic from a feudal state.

"We found a real-life parallel," declared a member of the production crew. "Our story, set a half century in the past, matched the current political situation as we experienced it, with Chinese revolutionaries again fighting a warlord, Red China, for an independent republic. Later, when we moved on to Hong Kong to film our 1926 street action we found ourselves ducking bricks and tear gas in actual 1966 Hong Kong street fights! We lived and worked under military jurisdiction, filming on a location technically at war."

On November 22, 1965, the film officially began shooting on the island of Taiwan (formerly known as Formosa).

Based on the novel by Richard McKenna, *The Sand Pebbles* cast McQueen in the central role of Jake Holman, a moody, tough-minded sailor serving as chief engineer on a U.S. gunboat cruising China's Yangtze River. The boat's mission was to protect the lives of American missionaries; the crew was made up of an assorted group of misfits who called themselves San Pebbles. McQueen is a loner, misunderstood and denounced by his crewmates. As engineer, his job is to keep the gunboat's cranky steam engine operating at full capacity. He meets a young schoolteacher (Candy Bergen) at one of the port missions and, despite himself, comes to love her. He finally decides to leave the Navy and work with her in the war-torn Chinese heartland. Too late. Nationalist troops attack the mission. In a fatal rearguard action, Holman sacrifices his life to allow his girl and the other Americans to escape via the waiting gunboat. (Incidentally, this ending, while set in a different war, is almost identical to that of the famous Hemingway epic, *For Whom the Bell Tolls*, in which American Robert Jordan dies in holding off Franco's troops while Jordan's girl and his Spanish friends escape into the mountains.)

The producer/director of *The Sand Pebbles*, Robert Wise, who was responsible for McQueen's first screen appearance, recalled this fact between scenes in Taiwan. "I gave him a walk-on in *Somebody Up There Likes Me*. Steve was a kooky New York character in a beanie at the time. Far out. Then I saw him again not too much later on the Coast when I directed Neile in *This Could Be the Night*. I never dreamed I'd be working with him here in the Orient as the star of a multimillion-dollar production. But the truth is, the part of Jake Holman is ideal for him, a perfect fit. I've never seen an actor work with mechanical things the way Steve does. He learned everything about the ship's engine, just as Holman did in the script. His excitement with the engine was real. It comes across.

"The years of car and cycle racing paid off for him in this one. That's why the role fits him so well. Holman is a very strong individual who does not bend under pressure. Which is very much like Steve: He's desperately determined to maintain his own strong identity. That comes *first* with him."

Others members of the cast sometimes found McQueen's intense individualism difficult to accept. Co-star Richard Crenna, who played the ship's captain, declared that "when I first talked to him his jargon was so odd it was like conversing with a Zulu warrior. Later we got along okay. But he's extremely cautious about friendship, about allowing people to enter his life. You have to sustain a relationship on *his* terms."

Steve was shocked by the number of homeless, underfed young girls wandering the Formosan streets—as was Robert Wise—and they decided to do something about the situation. They each contributed $12,500 to a missionary priest in Taiwan, Father Edward Wojnaik, enabling him to buy land on which to build a home for impoverished young women.

Shooting pool (at Green Beret headquarters) and biking provided Steve with between-scenes recreation. To keep his body in peak physical shape, he had five heavy crates of gym equipment imported from California and set up his own workout area aboard the San Pablo, bolting a full-size boxer's body bag to the ceiling, then installing weights, pulleys and barbells.

His wife approved of the miniature gym. "Steve works out at least three times a week no matter where we are," she stated. "If he can't find a regular gym to use he'll build his own, as he's done here. He's quite proud of his body."

McQueen is also proud of his gun collection and impressed Wise with his weapons expertise in the film. "He's the best actor I've ever worked with in the handling of guns," Wise flatly declared after Steve had completed a scene in which he defends a mission as a kind of one-man army, using several large weapons (rapid-fire rifles, etc.) to stunning effect.

Steve's zest for guns had caused him a bit of trouble when he first disembarked in the Orient. He'd arrived with a .38 police revolver in his suitcase. Customs officers quickly took it from him and locked the gun away, promising to send it back to him in the States. ("I guess they just didn't appreciate foreigners from Hollywood packing thirty-eights in their territory.")

In California McQueen keeps a select firearms collection in his den—a working assortment of some two dozen handguns, dueling pistols and rifles. Asked why he had gathered such a store of weapons, he pointed out that the urge to own a weapon goes back millions of years in man's history. "But I have no real interest in the death that guns deal out. I'm fascinated by the way they are put together, by the machinery of guns and gunmaking. A prize handgun is a work of art, just as much so as the engine in a Grand Prix Ferrari."

Neile, too, had her spare-time interests during this period. While the two McQueen children attended school at the Naval base, Neile put her dancing talents to charitable use when she volunteered to entertain Chinese troops garrisoned on the island of Kinmen (Quemoy) off the coast of Red China. Flown in by copter, Neile danced for a cheering mass of servicemen in the KDC auditorium 600 feet underground.

"I had a ball," she said, "and they had a ball, and it all played beautifully. Dancing is never work for me; it's as natural as breathing."

Back on the island, Steve was not nearly as contented; his passion for speed was totally frustrated in the Orient. One morning, while Neile was still on Kinmen, Steve rented a touring car with a driver who knew the island and took off for a run over Taiwan's narrow roads (mostly dirt and ambling cow paths). Steve's excursion was cut short by Taiwanese police, who waved the car to a halt and blamed McQueen's guide for allowing the American to exceed local speed limits.

"It's not *his* fault," Steve protested. "I'm the one to blame."

They sputtered and fumed, unable to decide on a course of action. Did the wild American intend to go on speeding in this mad fashion, or would he agree to slow down?

Steve smiled and responded by unfolding a small bicycle from the trunk of the touring car. He climbed aboard, smiled again, and pedaled slowly away, leaving the police speechless. ("I biked all the way back to the hotel—at a top speed of eight miles per hour.")

There were other frustrations. . . . The three months of location stretched out to six, as the cast and crew struggled against language barriers, tropical insects, disease, political turmoil and torrential monsoon rains. The tides of Taiwan, on which much of the shooting depended, proved to be totally unpredictable, and the lack of available drinking water was also a severe problem. (Steve and Neile were both affected by the bad water, and McQueen suffered a weight loss due to illness.)

On-set problems also arose as McQueen was often required to memorize a half dozen complex scenes at one throw—a task which was not helped by the babble of a thousand extras, shouting Taiwanese, Mandarin and Cantonese.

The McQueens moved from their cramped little house outside Taipei in the rice fields of Taiwan to Hong Kong for the last weeks of shooting, only to face street riots and near-bombardments.

But *The San Pebbles* finally wound up, and Steve was paid a handsome sum ($650,000) for his co-starring services. He claimed it was "the roughest film I ever made. I had my skull twisted a couple of times, got sick, inhaled tear gas, worked myself dingy and ended up exhausted back in the States."

He also ended up with an Academy Award nomination as Best Actor for his superb work as Holman, the Sand Pebble whose laconic on-screen statement might well serve to describe Steve himself: "As long as you're good at somethin' they can't beat you down."

7

OF CIRCUITS AND SAND DUNES

McQueen's Grand Prix racing film, set to roll in the summer of 1966, was scuttled as a direct result of the months of extended location work on *The Sand Pebbles*. Steve needed rest; he needed time off in order to pull himself together after the long grind of the Orient. He was simply not able to fly away for a season of race-filming in Europe. Thus, in June, Jack Warner officially announced that *Day of the Champion* had been shelved.

Shortly after Steve and his family had arrived back in the States he had put them all into a camper (stocked with a couple of racing cycles) and headed into the wilds of Utah, Montana and Canada. They explored the country, camping under the stars near clear creeks and rivers, where Steve used his cycle to beat through wooded areas. ("We saw bear and deer, possum and water otter," said Neile. "We fished, discovered waterfalls and hidden lakes and woke under clear blue skies. It was a great way for all of us to cleanse our souls after those endless monsoon months in the Orient.")

Steve's disappointment at not being able to make *Day of the Champion* was somewhat lessened that summer when he was invited to road-test an exotic variety of fast sports cars at California's Riverside Raceway for the Time/Life organization.

They had eight new models awaiting him at the circuit: a Jaguar 2 + 2 sedan, a V-8-engined Corvette Sting Ray, an Alfa Romeo Duetto Spyder, a Porsche 911, a Mercedes 230 SL, an Aston Martin DB6, a Shelby Cobra 427 and, the prize of the lot, a Ferrari 275 GTS.

It was Steve's joyous job to "wring them out" over the tough road circuit, then to comment on each car's performance for the readers of *Sports Illustrated*—a dream assignment, to which McQueen enthusiastically responded. He pulled on his crash helmet, strapped himself in the cockpit of his first choice (the Ferrari) and boomed away.

Each machine received a thorough test that afternoon as McQueen slammed first one car, then another around the demanding course; he didn't baby any of them. ("You don't find out anything by pussy-footing around a circuit.")

Of the Ferrari: "This one had more power than the model I own, which was nice. Steering was heavy at 20 mph, as it should have been, and became progressively lighter as I went faster. And shifting was a pleasure; Ferrari gearboxes shift like a knife through butter. The car was red-lined at 8,500 rpm, and I respected that limit—though I was doing 140 at one point. It was fun pushing her hard through the Esses. A wonderful car."

Of the Alfa Romeo: "With only 1,600-cc in the four-cylinder engine it was a bit underpowered for my liking. I was, however, very impressed with the brakes. I stopped six or seven times from 90 with absolutely no fade or locking. And it handled. Going through the first turn in fourth, at 7,000 rpm, I tried to break the rear end loose and couldn't. I finally got it skating by throwing it left, then right. A very forgiving machine."

Of the Mercedes: "Again, too underpowered to suit me. I look for more beans in the pot. I drove hard and got her out of shape a bit, but she behaved very nicely and never tried to bite me. An outstanding lady's car."

Of the Porsche: "The first Porsche I raced, my 1600 Super, had that violent oversteer tendency found in all the older models. They'd swap ends on you with no warning in a tight curve; you'd be all hung out and locked into the groove with nowhere to go. But this new 911 proved that Porsche had corrected the oversteer problem. This one was very neutral-handling, very docile, very pleasant to drive."

Of the Jaguar: "The automatic transmission was sluggish—and I much prefer a stick—but there's a great appeal in this one for the man who will accept a compromise. He can put his two kids in the back, his wife next to him in the front, and take off for a sporty vacation. A lot of car for the price. Neile was rather keen on it."

Of the Aston Martin: "It needed wider rims to get more meat on the road. Also, the seat design needed changing; I had to hold on to the door with one hand while going around corners. And when I shifted up from fourth to fifth at top revs the engine seemed to lose all its steam. A gentleman's auto."

Of the Corvette: "A brute. A terribly quick machine, very impressive. I liked it better than any of the lot, excepting the Ferrari. The V-8 made it really jump. Somebody accidentally turned on a sprinkler near turn one and there was suddenly some water on the track. I was boring in at 120, saw it, kind of got on tippytoes when I hit it, eased through, then got back on power right away to clear the tires. No problems. No panic. GM has done a great job in making these cars handle. I was once asked to race an old-model Corvette but passed because it handled so badly. This one sticks to the road."

Of the Cobra: "Brutal acceleration, with brakes to match. But under hard driving the gas would slosh to one side of the carburetor bowl on a tight turn and starve out the engine, and my knees cried ouch because of the seating position. Still, it's a real stoplight bandit."

The attention Steve garnered from this car-test session at Riverside led to another offer, this time from *Popular Science*, involving tests on dirt-and-desert cycles. McQueen agreed to take six fast bikes out to a desert scrambles course and twist the tiger's tail for *PS* readers. He selected a BSA 650-cc Hornet, a four-stroke 750-cc TT Norton-Metisse, a 650-cc Triumph Bonneville, a Honda 450, a Montesa La Cross and a Greeves-Challenger 250-cc two-stroke.

In the piece he wrote, Steve mentioned the advantage of being partners with Bud and Dave Ekins in their San Fernando Valley cycle shop, calling them "two of the best desert bike riders this country has ever produced."

McQueen picked out a scrambles course of six-mile perimeter, embracing sand washes, rocks, washboard-type dips and high-speed jumps. "Cow-trailing with a top close to 70 mph was possible over the faster portions," said Steve. "So the bikes got a really good workout."

He began with the BSA Hornet, which he called "a keen bike, but awfully heavy." He liked the special air cleaner, which he claimed was "important for the longevity of the engine because you don't have to take the carb apart to get out the sand and grit."

The Norton-Metisse, with its potent 750-cc engine, was "a handful, with loads and loads of torque, but more of a TT or track-riding bike because of its shorter forks which give less ground clearance than I like a scrambler to have."

The Honda he called "a very good bike for the money," and he praised the durability of the Greeves. "I've raced against them and they don't break down even in the hot, baked desert air, where a two-stroke is affected lots more than a four-stroke. Despite the quality of the two-stroke engine, I still didn't feel I had all the torque I needed to get out of trouble."

McQueen did, in fact, get into trouble when he tested the two-stroke Spanish Montesa and missed a fast corner. "I was in fourth gear and honking right along when I suddenly began to slide. I was committed to a line and just went flat out completely off the course. I expected to be up on the front end any second doing a swordfight in the air with the handlebars. There were some bad ruts, and I was really bouncing around out there. But the suspension took the punishment, and I found it easy to keep the weight going the way I wanted. This Montesa was quite forgiving in the rough."

Of the six bikes, Steve naturally favored the 650-cc Triumph Bonneville, a type of machine he'd competed on many times in the past. The new unit construction on this test model appealed to him. "Lately the lightweights have been nipping at its tail, but my feeling has been that the Triumph is best for competition desert riding. It is very strong and has more wins to its credit in desert events than any other bike."

Steve discussed his own hybrid, a competition cycle he had set up with the help of Bud and Dave Ekins: "The power is like supersonic! We used a big 650-cc Triumph four-stroke in a special light Rickman-Metisse frame. We cut down weight by eliminating the conventional oil tank. The frame itself, hollow, is the oil tank. Which has advantages. The oil circulates through the tubes of the frame and keeps cool. We also used Ceriani forks and fiber glass fenders, with a Triumph drive train and gearbox. The fork-crown was from a BSA. All in all, a neat package."

While Steve was busily testing cars and cycles that summer, Neile (who'd been encouraged by the reception accorded her dancing in the Orient) starred in a stock revival of *Pajama Game*. "Of course I'd done the show many times on Broadway," she said. "Which is when I first met Steve, so it was a kind of homecoming for me."

The two McQueen children enjoyed watching their mother sing and dance on stage, but by the second week of the engagement Steve began to miss her at home. He got "a little uptight"—and Neile once again put away her dancing shoes. Steve relaxed; he had his old lady back.

A close family friend explained his attitude: "Steve feels naked without Neile around. She's his shield. With her at his side he can cope, he can face what he considers to be a basically hostile world. Steve is stubborn, innately distrustful and overly sensitive to real or imagined slights. Strangers bug him. He hates glad-handers. However—and this is an important part of his nature—he is vitally concerned with the underdog, with people who have not been given a fair shake by society. He identifies with them, tries to help them."

Several times a year, without fanfare or publicity, McQueen loads up the family panel truck with food, blankets and medical supplies and drives out to the Four Corners area of Arizona, personally delivering these needed items to the starving Navajo Indians who live in this desolate part of the country. He has combined his star power with the prestige of Dr. Herman Salk, the Palm Springs veterinarian who is Jonas Salk's brother, to gather vital vaccines and antibiotics for the Navajos. ("I appreciate these people. They have an old saying they live by, concerning 'a land where there is time enough and room enough'—which is what we *all* need.")

Steve also shares a common passion for land preservation. In line with this, he narrated a conservation film that season, *The Coming of the Roads*. Additionally, his successful work with youngsters at the Boys Republic led to his being appointed to a board member's post on the Advisory Council of the Youth Studies Center at the

University of Southern California. ("Going to the first meeting kind of spooked me; I'd never even set foot on a college campus up to then!")

Before leaving for a New York world premiere of *The Sand Pebbles,* the McQueens hosted a lavish catered party in their Brentwood home. Steve's superstar pals James Garner and Paul Newman knocked elbows with Bud Ekins and other racing buddies. The party was a success, and Steve enjoyed himself, though he drank very little. ("I'm not a boozer. A beer now and again is about as far as I go. And all those Hollywood finger-poppin' parties are a bore for me. That's not my route.")

Steve talked about friendship: "This is a tough business. You take a man off the street and make him famous and he loses all sense of values. It's easy to take the full ride into Candyland. That's why it's important to have the right kind of friends, people who dig you for what you really are, for what you can deliver as a human being. They keep my head straight. I've only got a few like that, people I'm tight with. We see eye to eye on the basics."

Steve kept moving up. By the end of 1966 he'd signed a six-picture pact with Warner Brothers (all to be co-produced with his Solar company). And although he was not to receive an Oscar for *The Sand Pebbles,* his nomination was impressive in itself. Many other honors were coming his way: He received the *Photoplay* Gold Medal Award that year ("I didn't get a gold medal over in Germany but I finally got one in Hollywood!") and he was cited by the Foreign Press Association as "World Film Favorite." Japan's theater owners declared him to be "the most popular foreign star" for the second year running. Steve's price per picture had now climbed well above the $700,000 mark.

As one critic remarked: "College students respond to McQueen as a man of the moment. He represents the contemporary rebel, fighting to maintain an individual

85

stance in a computer-dominated society."

Critic/teacher Arthur Knight invited Steve to address his cinema class at USC in January, 1967. McQueen nervously agreed to appear.

Juggling questions from the students, Steve was asked how he picked one property over another in a sea of scripts.

"I have to be careful because my range is limited," he admitted. "There's a lot of stuff I just can't do, so I look for characters and situations that feel right to me. Even then, when I've got something that seems to fit, it's a hell of a lot of work. Every script is an enemy to conquer. I put a chunk of myself into each role. I see three scripts a day, and I take my time choosing the right one."

The vehicle Steve finally chose to follow *The Sand Pebbles* was a fast-paced crime caper in which he was to portray what he called "a rich dude who decides to goose the establishment." The title, at this point, was not decided (it was eventually released as *The Thomas Crown Affair*) although the locations were set: Boston and Cape Cod.

Before leaving on this new assignment Steve fidgeted through a United Jewish Welfare luncheon (where he was lauded for his contributions to the Boys Republic and the Youth Studies Center), pressed his footprints into the wet-concrete forecourt of Grauman's Chinese in Hollywood (the 153rd star to be so honored) and discussed a possible merchandising scheme with execs at Montgomery Ward (involving a special "McQueen motorcycle" with matching equipment).

"Man, I was glad to finally shake loose and head for Boston," he said. "By the time I got Neile and the kids all packed and on the way I was half out of my tree. Success can bug you as much as failure. Everybody was suddenly treating me like a superstar and I knew I was still the same as I'd always been. When I got that call for location I just *ran*."

In *The Thomas Crown Affair* a sated young Boston millionaire decides to engineer the "perfect" robbery. Not for profit, but strictly for the stimulation provided by such a venture. Thomas Crown thus masterminds a successful and spectacular robbery involving huge sums of company money. He soon finds himself in a mental battle with a tireless, equally brilliant female insurance investigator who is determined to tie him to the crime. The clash of wills between these two "beautiful people" and their eventual romantic entanglement forms the plot of this sardonic anti-establishment film.

When McQueen signed to essay the dapper, polo-playing Boston aristocrat there were those who doubted his ability to be convincing as a bored intellectual.

"At first I was advised not to do it," said Steve. "They told me it would be like trying to make a purse out of a sow's ear. But I said, wait a minute, this dude wants to show he can beat the establishment at its own game. He's essentially a rebel, like me. Sure, a high-society rebel, but he's *my* kind of cat. It was just his outer fur that was different—so I got me some fur."

Steve went to Beverly Hills tailor Ron Postal and spent many hours getting measured for custom tuxedoes and $350 suits. He replaced his scuffed loafers with hand-crafted Italian shoes. A selection of contoured silk shirts and Boston ties completed the "outer fur."

No one was more pleased with the dapper new McQueen image than his wife. ("Neile said I looked like a gentleman for the first time in my life.")

But one item was missing. . . .

"Tommy Crown wears a Phi Beta Kappa key across his vest," said Steve. "I needed one. I finally borrowed our set designer's key. Now all I had to do was climb behind the wheel of Crown's big Rolls and I was home."

Faye Dunaway, the dynamic actress from *Bonnie and Clyde*, co-starred as the sexy insurance girl, and one scene called for an extended kissing-biting love bit between Faye and Steve. As director Norman Jewison shot the sequence, it consumed eight hours of set work—a full day's shooting. After so much kissing and nibbling Steve admitted that his lips were "sore for the whole weekend" and that Neile "wasn't exactly overjoyed at the scene."

Faye Dunaway was asked about McQueen, about what kind of person he was. "He's for real," she said. "He's willing to do things other stars just wouldn't dare try. He's a risk-taker and that cutting edge of his comes across on film."

Steve, in turn, was equally impressed with Faye. He seldom gave out comments on his co-stars, yet broke his rule on this occasion: "She's good people, a tough in-the-trench fighter who works hard and makes *you* work hard. A real pro."

In one of their many scenes together Steve and Faye engage one another in a brilliant, classically correct chess game. Move by move, it was based on an actual game played by experts Zeissl and Walthoffen in Vienna in 1899. ("Which is how come we looked so brilliant!")

Polo was one of the new skills Steve had to master while he was on location. Although he'd done a good deal of riding in the *Wanted* TV series and in the Westerns he'd made, McQueen had never sat an English saddle (nor had he competed on horseback).

"I wasn't used to that saddle," he admitted. "The first time the horse stopped quick I was right up on his neck hanging onto his ears. Polo is rugged. I was three weeks learning the game. I'd get to the field two or three hours before the morning's shooting just to practice. I got polo blisters over my bike blisters learning to stay aboard a polo pony."

He didn't always manage to stick in the saddle; a polo pony is guided by knee pressure. ("The horse was a lot smarter than I was. He knew the game and I didn't. He'd go left—and I'd go right, flat on my ear. But I finally got the hang of it and began having fun batting down the field.")

All of the polo sequences were shot at the elite Myopia Hunt Club near Hamilton, Massachusetts, where McQueen marveled, "Imagine me riding against these social biggies like Adam Winthrop and Crocker Snow. Their blueblood must run back three hundred years!"

Steve explained the roots of the sport: "It originated in Mongolia—and polo means *poolo,* which is Mongolian for 'skull.' They'd take a human skull, toss it into the middle of a field and all the riders from two towns would come out with long sticks. Whoever could bat the skull into the other town first won the women and the wine of that town. The English came up with the civilized version."

Sky-gliding was another sport which Steve was required to learn for *Crown.* The story had originally called for sky-diving, but McQueen and Jewison substituted gliding since it seemed more in keeping with *Crown*'s character. Sky-gliding, for a Boston blueblood, was a more socially acceptable pastime.

McQueen learned to handle a glider well enough to satisfy Jewison. "But," admitted Steve, "once I missed the field I was aiming for, where they had the cameras set up for my landing. Instead, I ended up in a potato patch. Only my ego was damaged."

Several action scenes involved the use of a special souped-up high-speed dune buggy which Steve had helped build (with the aid of California's talented Pete Condos). When the machine was shipped out to the sand dunes at Cape Cod for location shots Steve was somewhat dubious about its potential: "We'd used a shortened VW chassis and a fiber glass body shell into which we'd stuffed a hairy Corvair turbo-charged 180-hp job with four two-barrel down-draft carbs. It *looked* great, and it was all right once you got it locked into the lip of a 190-foot sand bowl. You could drift the lip at 75 or 80, smooth as anything, just kind of piddling the wheel to keep her in line. Or you could get the front end straight up in the air and just squirt along on the rear wheels for a while. But with all the torque you felt like someone was gripping your skin and pulling it back around your face. And no roll bar. If it flipped you could get your melon rearranged. Mostly, though, you just rolled out in the sand."

What concerned McQueen was the machine's basic understeer tendency and the fact that the linkage wires would get clogged with sand and jam the throttle wide open. Which happened more than once.

"Faye was riding with me for all those dune scenes," said Steve. "I figure she should have been awarded the Purple Heart for doing it. We had these two fat Indy-type tires on the back, which made the thing understeer something fierce. And we did one big jump for the camera right off the edge of a high dune. It was wild, with the rear wheels clappin' each other in the air. Those VW rear ends, if you get 'em airborne, they just clap hands. Faye was hangin' on like crazy, gritting her teeth. The back of the floorboard was scratched raw from her heels, where she tried to find some traction down there!"

The understeer problem manifested itself in one dramatic sequence near the ocean. Jewison had told Steve to head the sleek orange bug down the beach at speed, to head straight for the water and then, at the last second, to spin the buggy at the edge of the surf. "It'll make a great shot," he told Steve.

With Faye braced beside him, at 6,500 rpm, McQueen roared over the packed sand, aimed for the ocean, engine howling. So far so good. Now it was time to spin the buggy.

"I wrestled with the wheel and nothing happened," recalled McQueen. "The thing just wouldn't steer. We kept heading right for the lousy ocean at a terrific rate of speed. Well, on the filmed rushes, all you could see was this orange bug disappearing into the water. I thought I'd drowned my co-star, but Faye came out of it soaked and smiling. Some gal. They had to take the entire engine apart, strip it down, to get the saltwater out. Cost $700 for that unscheduled dip in the briny."

There were also some family problems to solve while Steve was making *Crown*. The McQueens had rented a house for the summer in an upper-middle-class suburb of Boston, with the idea that a "real home" would give their two children a sense of proportion and that they would feel less uprooted.

"However," reported Neile, "it didn't work out too well. Terry made friends with some children old enough to know who Steve was, and our quiet was suddenly shattered. All of the neighborhood kids began to descend on us, constantly after Steve for autographs or attention whenever he was home. He caused a real hubbub, and for the first time the children began to realize that their father was someone special. And that made *them* start to feel and act special, which was wrong. We didn't want them to lose their sense of balance. It's so easy to spoil a Hollywood child. That summer in Boston frightened us; it showed us how difficult it would be to keep our children's lives from becoming distorted. That's when we decided to allow them to live at home in Brentwood during the filming of Steve's next picture."

The next one was a real cinema classic, destined to break box office records from the first week of its release; Steve McQueen was about to make one of the most dangerous and exciting films of his career—the tough, lean, superswift thriller called *Bullitt*.

8

THE GREAT SAN FRANCISCO CAR CHASE

"We've got a downtown homicide," the cool radio voice crackled, naming the site of the crime. "Better get right over there."

"Roger," replied the police cruiser. "We're on the way."

Cutting in his siren, the driver swung the heavy patrol car around a sharp corner and headed for Market Street. Seated beside him, making mental notes of the exact procedures involved, Steve McQueen frowned. "That's the fourth homicide this weekend, isn't it?"

"Fifth," corrected the driver. "Sometimes they come in bunches."

Steve had been riding San Francisco squad cars as an observer for almost a week. He'd obtained an official clearance from the city's police chief as part of the extensive reseach undertaken for his portrayal of Frank Bullitt, a hard-nosed San Francisco police detective.

Steve's first reaction, prior to accepting the role, was one of severe self-doubt. "I'd never expected to play a cop," he admitted. "As a kid, running the streets, I'd been hassled a lot by the police and I'd always figured that they were on one side of life with me on the other. I never felt easy around a cop. But here I was in 'Frisco, seeing the other side of police work, and it was a real eye-opener."

This was the first film on which McQueen exerted overall control; *Bullitt* was structured as a Solar production with Warner-7 Arts as the parent company bankrolling the package. Steve was, in effect, working for himself, and when it came to script and/or production decisions he had the final word. Which is why Peter Yates of England (who had never done a film in the United States) was chosen to direct. Yates was signed on the strength of his realistic car-chase sequences from his British production of *Robbery*. A very wild, potentially dangerous car chase had been written into *Bullitt* (at McQueen's suggestion) and it would take an experienced directing hand to bring it off properly.

When Kenneth Hyman, the executive in charge of production for Warner's, found out about the planned bang-about over San Francisco streets he attempted to have the action switched to the studio lot where it could be "safely controlled."

Yates and McQueen flatly rejected this idea; authenticity was at stake. Skidding around a phony studio street and bouncing off rubber-padded curbs just wouldn't get the job done.

"We wanted a gut-buster," said McQueen. "That meant we had to do it on location, using real streets. I huddled with chassis designer Max Balchowsky and we worked out some modifications for the two cars involved in the action: a new 390 GT Mustang (which we figured a cop like Bullitt could afford to own) and a 440 Magnum Dodge Charger for the bad guys to drive."

Balchowsky's main job was to prepare these cars to

withstand the incredible beating they'd take as they were banged down, up and around San Francisco's steep-plunging hills. Suspension systems were heavily beefed. On the Mustang, Koni shocks and heavy-duty coil springs were used. The mounts were reinforced and a cross-beam milled heads and reworked carbs. The Charger's torsion bars were shortened and the lower arms reinforced. NASCAR springs were added on the rear, as well as special Bonneville shocks. Both cars were fitted with disc brakes and wrap-around interior roll bars.

"After five weeks of work," said McQueen, "Max had 'em ready and Bill Hickman and I took the cars out to Cotati Raceway. We needed to find out what they'd do in the way of handling, braking and acceleration. Hickman is an old stunt pro and it was decided that he would actually drive the Charger in our film, playing the baddie, while I chased him as Frank Bullitt in the Mustang."

In the beginning, San Francisco officials took a dim view of the proposed auto chase through the streets of their city. "We got tossed out of the mayor's office the first time we tried to get his okay," admitted Steve. "They thought we were out to make the cops look bad."

Things smoothed over when McQueen carefully explained that the film was not, in any manner, anti-police, nor would the car chase take up more than a very small part of the action. "So they agreed to block off some streets for us, but they didn't realize just *what* we would be doing with those cars! Even we didn't know how wild it was gonna get!"

Locations for the chase included several of the steepest hills within the city and incorporated a very fast waterfront run, followed by a full-throttle bash along a speedy turnpike beyond the city in which the chase climaxed in a spectacular spinout and explosive crash.

"I'd always had a yen to see a car hit a gas station and blow up," said McQueen. "In a film, I mean. So we had this written into the end of the chase: The Charger shoots off the highway into this filling station and, blambo! the whole shebang blows sky-high!"

Several top stunt men were employed to ensure total realism, but since McQueen was boss he planned to do all of his own stunt driving, a decision no studio producer would have approved.

"Neile always worries about my racing," he said. "So I just didn't tell her about this chase. She was down in Los Angeles with our kids, and I figured what she didn't know wouldn't upset her."

A special flat-bed V-8-powered camera car was used (actually a stripped-down Can-Am Chevy transaxle) in which veteran cameraman Bill Fraker filmed most of the hazardous action. Cameras were mounted on the nose of Steve's car in order to capture the stomach-wrenching, heart-in-the-mouth moments when the black Mustang would soar over the cliff-steep brow of a hill, bottom with a great metallic crunch, then roar straight down in tire-smoking pursuit of Hickman's fleeting Dodge.

There were four cars used in *Bullitt*, since a back-up model was provided for each machine. These "doubles" were also competition prepared. If one car was vitally damaged the back-up model was there to fill in for the cameras. (As it turned out, the doubles were very necessary indeed!)

Preparations for the chase were moving into their final preshooting phase on the morning Steve received a special-delivery letter from Warner's Ken Hyman. It specified that until the film's completion McQueen was forbidden to ride his motorcycle to and from the set. The studio would provide safe transportation. An agreement form was enclosed for his signature.

"I was plenty annoyed," Steve declared. "Instead of signing the form I scrawled something vulgar across it and sent it back. Nobody, at this point, had the legal right to keep me off my bike. Actually, when you think about it, the whole thing was highly ironic."

He referred to the irony of being asked not to ride a cycle to a location in which he was to risk his neck flinging a race-prepared Mustang through city streets at speeds in excess of 100 miles an hour. Hollywood irony.

Since practice runs were impossible, no one in the company knew quite what to expect in the way of problems during that first morning on the hills of San Francisco. The side streets had been roped off by police equipped with walkie-talkies, and several stunt drivers had lined up ahead of the normal street traffic, keeping a four-way intersection clear for the slam-bang run.

"Okay, roll 'em!" shouted Yates—and with a gutteral roar of exhaust Hickman cannoned down the hill in the Dodge, McQueen hard after him. Trailing them both, driven with equal vigor, was the V-8 Chevy, Fraker grinding away with his camera.

A newsman described the scene: "Suddenly, here's the Charger, the Mustang and the Chevy, all careening through the intersection at top speed, making a tremendous racket, squalling rubber and screaming away up the next hill and out of sight. Pedestrians were in a state of shock!"

Stopping the cars after such desperate sprints was a problem in itself, as McQueen related. "We did have some trouble shutting down out of camera range since both the Mustang and the Charger were fairly rigid. We'd panic brake from 80 or 90 and the back end would start chattering, and those Firestone F-100 radials would be jumpin' and smokin'. It took awhile to get things under control."

Usually a single run at a location was the rule, since the thundering parade of racing machinery always drew instant crowds, which made subsequent runs extremely risky.

"Sometimes we'd go twice," said Steve, "but most of the

time we'd have to grab our footage on the first shot and split. We couldn't keep an eye on everybody, couldn't hold 'em all out of range. The realism was spoiled if there were too many people around. It had to look ordinary, with the normal number of pedestrians on the streets."

McQueen found that bulling a stock car through flat intersections after a furious downhill run required a special technique. Even his extensive track experience had not prepared him for this unique style of driving.

"There was one scene where I was supposed to swing fast around a narrow side street and clip a parked car. The thing is, we were *really* going to just kind of ding this guy's car and leave a note on the window telling him to ring Warner's to have the damage repaired. Anyhow, when I finally took the corner I overcooked it completely and smashed right into the parked car, just wrote it off and bounced into another one next to it. We got a bit more realism than we'd bargained for."

Bill Hickman also had his problems. On a fast run, halfway down the hill, the Charger's foot pedal suddenly snapped dead to the floor. No brakes! Always the cool professional, Hickman threw the Dodge into a tire-shrieking broadslide, barely making the corner at the bottom of the hill. (He also barely missed the assembled police and production crew.)

"Bill did wipe out one of our cameras," said McQueen. "We left that piece of footage in the final print. You can see it on the screen. The Dodge comes round, slides right into the audience and everything suddenly goes red for a split second. That was our camera blowing up!"

In all, eight cameras were employed to cover the action. Two of them were mounted inside the cars, both 35-mm units, using 200-foot magazines and painted black so they would not be detected.

The punishment which each car suffered went far

beyond what even McQueen or Balchowsky had imagined. The dead-flat intersections at the bottom of each plunging hill took their toll.

"Every time I'd hit an intersection," Steve recalled, "my oil sump would ground heavily on the street. I'd hear this loud 'thwack bang' noise inside the car. I'd pull over, get out, and sure enough the sump would be cracked wide open and all the oil gone. We'd clean up the street, bolt on another sump, pour in fresh oil and take off again."

Mechanics were quick to check out both cars after the end of each run, since a broken spindle or a loose wheel could have had fatal results. And each night the crew would gather with a stack of city maps and a blackboard to plot out the following day's action. Then, early the next morning, Steve would receive his wake-up call at the hotel and be told where the crew wanted him to appear for shooting.

"This went on for two weeks," said McQueen. "And I did all my own stunt driving during that period. Then one morning I didn't get my call and overslept. When I woke up I didn't know what was happening. I phoned around, found out where the crew was shooting and took my bike over there—only to see ole Bud Ekins coming down a hill for the cameras in my Mustang, wearing my jacket and sunglasses. I rushed over to Pete Yates and Bob Relyea, who was our producer, and began yelling bloody murder. They told me, very gently, to shut up and go sit down because I wasn't *about* to do any hill jumps for these final runs. Which is when I found out the full story. . . ."

It seems that a family friend of the McQueens had innocently described Steve's full-throttle driving to Neile back in Los Angeles. She'd immediately phoned Relyea, begging him to keep her car-happy husband out of the Mustang for the final steep Chestnut Street hill jumps. Relyea had agreed and had called in Bud Ekins to sub for

Steve. Informed of Neile's worried state of mind, Steve backed down and allowed his old bike buddy to complete the dangerous hill sequences.

Ekins described the hill-jump sensation as "like driving off the end of the world. I'd hit the intersection at 60, bottom, then take off for a thirty-foot jump. The landing was critical because I knew that if a wheel dug in and the car started flipping it would have barrel-rolled all the way to the bottom. No way I could have survived." (Ekins could not wear a crash helmet since he was doubling for a detective in street clothing.)

By the completion of the hill runs both cars needed extensive repairs, particularly the Mustang. The door handles came adrift and both front shocks were broken, as was the steering armature on the right side. Also, the engine mountings were loose. As McQueen got out of the Mustang, after a final closeup take, the entire door fell off. ("It looked like a circus act!")

Crew mechanics effected the necessary repairs, getting the cars ready for the waterfront and high-speed turnpike segments. Neile hadn't known about these and no promises had been made to her about keeping Steve out of this action. Thus, Ekins went back to his cycles and McQueen again took over the Mustang.

"The level runs were as wild as the hill stuff," said Steve. "Here was Bill Fraker hangin' out of that stripped-down racing Chevy, sittin' on a chair with his camera stuck out there at 114 miles per hour right down the city street about six feet away from me while I drove flat out with cement standards whippin' past us. . . ."

On the highway section near the waterfront, with both cars blasting along at top revs, paced by Fraker in the V-8, an old man in a dusty passenger sedan missed a shouted police command and putt-putted into the scene at a sedate 25 miles per hour. ("Somehow," declared a shaken observer, "there was no collision—just one very scared old man.")

The first section of the turnpike run involved car-to-car bumping at high speed, and Peter Yates was personally responsible for much of this footage; he rode in the backseat of the Mustang, using a hand-held camera to record it.

Police had closed off this fast section of freeway and all of the "traffic" in these scenes consisted of company vehicles driven by stunt men. The action called for Hickman to graze the side of a truck, bounce into a guard rail and then engage McQueen in a savage car-bashing contest—during which the two machines, roaring along side by side at over 100, would bang into one another, each trying to force the other off the road.

Steve admired his director's nerve. "Pete is quite a guy," he declared. "I was really belting the Mustang along, but ole Pete was back there yellin' for more speed. Or for me to clout Bill's car harder!"

At one point in the chase a shotgun blast from the villain's car blows out McQueen's front windshield (carefully rigged to shatter *out*ward). At another point a frightened motorcycle rider panics at seeing the two cars bear down on him, slides out of control and takes a long skidding fall directly in the Mustang's path.

Steve elaborated on this latter sequence: "Bud Ekins was the rider, and when he told us he was going to do this stunt I really didn't want him to do it. 'You're liable to get kissed off and your wife'll never forgive me,' I told him. But he was stubborn, convinced he could do it okay, so we let him go ahead. Man, I'll tell you, I never saw anything as scary as having him throw that BSA down in front of us. He must have slid at least seventy-five feet along the blacktop. I just twisted the Mustang sideways to miss him, spun twice and slapped the bank—which wasn't in the script!"

The automotive mayhem was not yet done; the gas station blowup remained as a final, fiery climax to the chase and this took detailed preparation: Dummy pumps were constructed for the Dodge to hit, and nitro charges were carefully rigged. McQueen's Mustang would appear to force the Dodge into the station, and at the moment of impact an explosives expert would trigger the nitro to simulate the exploding pumps. Car and station would erupt into gouts of raw flame. The timing, at each stage, had to be exact, and once the station blew there was no retake possible.

"We had Carey Loftin dressed in my jacket driving the Mustang for this end sequence," said Steve. "Loftin's been doing movie stunts for half his life. A real veteran. He even worked on trick stuff with W. C. Fields way back in the thirties. There's almost nothing he can't do. Anyhow, we had him come down the highway, side-towing the Charger. The two cars *looked* as if they were still racing. Then he had to work a quick-release gimmick at just the right second, sending the Dodge across the road into the gas pumps. At which point the nitro goes and we've got our scene."

The sequence was almost a fiasco. The Dodge took longer to cross the highway than expected and missed the pumps to smash directly into the station. But the special effects man triggered the nitro, and the station blew on schedule.

"In the film," said McQueen, "if you watch *real* close, you can see the Dodge overshoot the pumps. But it all came out fine."

The chase ends with Steve's Mustang wiping across four lanes of traffic and spinning itself to a dusty standstill in a ditch. Steve tried it more than once and just could not spin the Mustang on cue.

"It went against my grain as a racing driver," he explained. "To deliberately spin a car is very tough. My instincts are set against it. So Carey took over, put small tires on the Mustang, and went out there and spun her for the cameras on the first take, neat as you please.

"Which wrapped up our great San Francisco car chase. It had consumed three weeks. It took that much hot driving to get our nine minutes of final footage, but it sure was worth the time and trouble. We all realized we'd pulled off something really special."

McQueen personally involved himself in one other risky stunt sequence for *Bullitt*, this one filmed at the San Francisco airport at 3:30 a.m. on a cold, windy morning in April. The script action called for Steve to leap from a stationary passenger jet in pursuit of a killer, sprint across the dark midfield runway area and, as a Pan American 707 is taking off, throw himself under the wing as the huge liner blasts over him, then hop up to resume his foot chase.

Neile, who had flown from Los Angeles to be on hand for the shooting, was asked if watching such stunts made her nervous. "Of course," she nodded. "But Steve asked me to come, so I'm here. He's rehearsed everything and knows just what he's doing."

Director Yates raised a hand to the pilot of the waiting 707. A moment of suspense—then the "roll 'em" order was given and the big plane began to move. As it gathered speed, Steve sprinted directly toward it from the opposite side of the runway. The fan-jet engines sent out a deafening blast of sound as McQueen ducked expertly under the moving wing, slamming himself to the runway in time to escape the 240-degree surge of furnace heat from the moving jet pods.

"The vibration tweaked my neck a bit," he said afterward. "When you hit the deck you've got to open your mouth and hold your ears. It blew me around a little but I'm okay. How'd it look?"

Yates assured him it looked great.

Neile remained in town that weekend. She was now bringing the children to be with their father on Saturdays and Sundays, and they had rented a penthouse apartment overlooking San Francisco Bay, where Steve enjoyed watching the boats through a high-power telescope Neile had given him for his birthday.

Terry's birthday gift was a string of "hippie love beads" for Steve to wear around his neck. He liked them so much he actually considered using the beads in a trade ad for *Bullitt*. ("Love beads and a gun, as a symbol of the hip detective.")

"We'd drive over the bridge to Sausalito on Sundays," said Neile. "Steve was working hard and needed such outings. It was fun for all of us."

As a result of mounting costs, Warner-7 Arts decided to terminate their agreement with McQueen. By May costs had climbed past five million and, the studio called off its deal on all future Solar productions; McQueen would have to find another parent financing company.

"We didn't worry about that," said Steve. "We all knew we had a hit in *Bullitt*. Nobody closely connected with the film ever doubted it would make big money. Even the local cops dug it!"

Steve had screened a rough cut print for the chief of police and other San Francisco officials, all of whom enjoyed the picture. At this showing, McQueen made a solid impression on several city detectives when he demonstrated his skill in a specialized form of Chinese hand combat at the Department of Justice. (Watching him, one detective declared: "This guy is really *sudden*.")

City officials were also pleased when Steve donated a swimming pool to the recreation park in San Francisco's impoverished Hunter's Point district. ("The kids needed a place to swim, so I provided one. No big deal. Just a thing I wanted to do.")

By June the McQueens were in Las Vegas. To "cool out" after *Bullitt*, Steve had entered the Stardust 7-11, one of the roughest competitive events on the racing calendar. As Steve described it: "This is a lot like road racing—only without a road."

9

OFF THE ROAD AND ON THE TRACK

Steve's dune buggy experience in *The Thomas Crown Affair* had whetted his taste for such vehicles, and after spectating at an off-road event at Hemet (a scramble for modified four-wheelers over ungraded terrain) McQueen entered the family jeep in a similar go at Riverside.

The affair was held in a sand wash in which a wicked dip over a three-foot-deep stand of water formed part of the fun. Steve had gunned his Chevy jeep up to 70 when he got sideways into the dip, bumped and jounced about until the hood popped up. ("I was suddenly blind with that big plastic hood sticking up in front of me. I ended stuck in the mud. Not a very impressive debut.")

However, that same weekend he tried out off-road designer Vic Hickey's Baja Boot—a racing special originally developed for moon-terrain travel, powered by a potent 450-hp engine.

"The Boot is a neat job," said Steve. "Basic space

frame, four-wheel drive automatic, independent suspension all-round. Drives as smooth as a Cadillac. It'll hit close to 100 over a sand wash, and in really rough country, across open desert, you can get it rolling at 60 or more, with a top of 135 on smooth highway."

McQueen subsequently arranged with Hickey to pilot the Boot in the Stardust 7-11 championship run out of Las Vegas in June, 1968, and Bud Ekins agreed to ride with Steve.

"To tell you the truth, I think the bikes are going to win this one," Steve commented before the race. "You sit up a lot higher on a bike and you can see farther out front. In a car, you're lower and can't spot the ditches. With a bike you can crank 'er up to 80, stand on the pegs, and just dance over most of the road hazards."

The hazards in the Mint 7-11 were severe enough to paralyze the ordinary motorist, yet no less than 137 entries were there that June to tackle the dusty Amargosa Desert with its varied terrors. The McQueen/Ekins Boot was entered in Class 6, for nonproduction four-wheel-drive vehicles. Entries were spread through eight classes in all, and these included Ford Broncos, Hondas, Volvos, VW's, Dodge pickups, Datsuns and Toyota Land Cruisers, as well as all manner of jeeps, dune buggies, cut-down specials and, of course, the racing cycles, twenty-three of them; this was their kind of race over their kind of country, and as McQueen predicted, the bikes would be hard to beat.

Sponsored by the National Off-Road Racing Association, this event was laid out over a huge, sprawling 320-mile loop, stretching down through Nevada along the California border, through hills and washes and dry lakes back to Las Vegas. Competitors were required to run two complete loops in order to win. The starting point was the Stardust Raceway outside Las Vegas.

Neile and Betty Ekins (Bud's wife) were there to cheer on their husbands; they walked beside the big red racing

Boot as it rolled slowly forward for its 12:06 start. The race was already well underway, with the smaller machines going off the line as early as 11 a.m.

Steve checked his shoulder harness, pulled down his goggles and turned to kiss Neile. "Don't forget the coffee. We'll be needing some by Ash Meadows."

"I won't forget," promised Neile.

Betty hugged Bud, and the two women stepped back, waving, as the Boot moved up to the line, its engine pulsing with harnessed power under McQueen's throttle foot. The flag snapped down, and the Boot roared into action with a plume of smoke from its fat tires.

Neile and Betty watched the Boot bump and batter its way over the raw-rock desert until the red blur faded along the dust-curtained horizon. "We'd best get started," said Betty. "It's a long drive to the checkpoint."

The wives had it easy. Their route took them over wide, smooth Nevada highways to "Checkpoint Charlie," near Ash Meadows, about 100 miles out from Las Vegas—but to reach this same point in the race Steve had to rip over the roadless washboard desert, run across the buttes to stateline, push on up along the California border over hills strewn with sharp, tire-slashing deposits of lava, bump through boulder-choked washes and forge two dry lakes filled with treacherous talcum-soft silt.

In the sun-blast of 100-degree heat, Neile and Betty waited through the long day for Steve and Bud to appear, but there was no sign of the red Boot.

Reports began filtering in to the checkpoint: A bike rider had unloaded in the rough and broken his wrist; a jeep was on fire; several machines had overturned and many more were bogged down or had broken their metal bodies fighting the rocky terrain.

As the exhausted, sunburned competitors struggled into the checkpoint Neile questioned them. Had anyone seen the Boot?

"Sure did, lady," nodded one jeep driver, swigging water, then wiping his dust-caked face with a damp towel. "I know for certain it passed stateline cuz I saw that red devil 'bout fifteen miles this side of the line goin' like hell's hammers. They should be along soon now."

But the Boot didn't show. The wives kept waiting as the sun dropped behind the mountains and the desert darkness closed in.

Before the race Steve had shrugged aside the dangers. "Okay, so I could maybe break a leg out there. But the odds are against anything more serious happening."

Actually Steve didn't break a leg; he broke an axle. At 9 p.m. word reached Neile and Betty: The Boot was stranded thirty-two miles out on a high rock dune with a wheel sheared. Both drivers were okay.

"It was the darndest thing," McQueen recalled. "We were really battin' along, feeling good about the car and our chances with it, when we see this big fat wheel rolling along beside us. It's *our* wheel! The axle had popped. Well, that did it. We sat on our tails in the desert till help came. As for the Mint, the bikes took it."

They did, indeed, finishing first, second, third and fourth. Their race. Their country. A prediction verified.

By October Steve was back on a cycle, doing "wheelies" on TV for the Ed Sullivan show, then taking Ed for a ride in a special McQueen-designed dune buggy.

This TV stint was strictly for publicity: In addition to his Solar film production unit McQueen was also seriously involved with Solar Engineering, a firm he'd organized to produce off-road vehicles, equipment and cycle kits, among other automotive products. The buggy on the Sullivan show was Solar-equipped, and Steve revealed that he was then in the process of working out a new safety seat for use in off-road machines.

"I got concerned when a friend of mine flipped his buggy and messed up his neck," stated McQueen. "So I got me a big hunk of clay, had some drawings made and worked out this seat, then had a rotational mold cast from the clay model and laid a special covering over it. We called it the Baja Bucket and began selling it to racing guys. I'm proud of the results. The Bucket has saved more than one life on a flip-over. We now use them ourselves on the Boot."

Steve was also putting some of his money into building a new beach house at Malibu. He had a house in the hills above Palm Springs, plus his "pad" in Brentwood, and now the beach place. As Neile remarked: "Usually actors with three houses have one in the States, one in New York or Connecticut and one on the Riviera. We're probably the only industry people who have three in the same place—all in southern California!"

Steve's next film, *The Reivers*, locationed in Mississippi and was based on William Faulkner's novel about a boy who learns the facts of life from a shiftless, happy-go-lucky character called Boon, a "reiver"—which is a period translation of rascal. McQueen was Boon, and the part called for him to "borrow" a spanking new 1905 Winton Flyer for a joy ride with the boy down the narrow dirt roads of the Deep South.

But where, in 1968, was Solar going to find a spanking new 1905 Winton?

"I went to my old pal, Von Dutch," said McQueen, "and I laid the problem on him. This cat can build anything from guns to tanks, and he agreed to supply our Winton. Made it all himself, from the frame up, out of old aluminum furnace sidings and God knows what else. When he showed it to us we all gasped. The thing was just beautiful—bright yellow, gleaming with polished brass—a perfect replica of a genuine 1905 Flyer, but with a modern power plant under the hood. We needed some kick on those Southern goat trails."

Before he uncorked the new-old Winton for the cameras Steve got a chance to power a stock racing car around the oval track in Carrollton, Mississippi. His brisk, dirt-sliding exhibition run in the stocker delighted the crowd. McQueen quietly declined an offer to enter the weekend stock car bash. ("Sorry, but I've got a 1905 Winton to drive.")

In the film Steve gets the Winton stuck in a mudhole and attempts to push it out. The scene was all too real: McQueen was totally covered in mud, nose to toes, before the scene ended.

Not all of the location work was done in the South; the climax of the picture, a comic, wildly exciting horse race, was filmed at the Walt Disney ranch back in California, and Steve returned home to find that he had once again cinched the *Photoplay* Gold Medal Award as Favorite Male Star of the year. In fact, by 1969, Steve's popularity soared to a record high: *Bullitt* not only won Solar an Oscar (for best film editing) but became one of the top five box office hits around the world.

McQueen was invited to London in June for a tribute by the Royal Academy of Dramatic Art, and that trip to Europe served a double purpose: He attended the Le Mans race in France with his Solar camera crew and captured 30,000 feet of "workhorse footage" for a projected film based on the famous twenty-four-hour international motor race.

Losing *Day of the Champion* still bothered him. Le Mans offered Steve a chance to fulfill an old dream. "For some while I'd had the idea of doing a picture at Le Mans," he said. "A kind of definitive treatment of automotive competition within a dramatic framework or, to put it more bluntly, I wanted to make the best damn racing movie ever!"

But he had trouble getting proper backing. "I couldn't convince the money men. They didn't understand what I wanted to do. Which is why I took my camera crew to the sixty-nine race. The footage we brought back would show the excitement, the drama. . . . Then, too, we wanted the officials at Le Mans to trust us. We wanted them to understand that we were pros who knew how to stay out of their way and who respected the sport and the race."

Steve admitted that he had not anticipated the actual tension and excitement of Le Mans until witnessing it. "The emotional buildup is fantastic. When the countdown started, with the long line of cars poised for their run in front of those jammed grandstands . . . well, you can *feel* the vibes."

Steve took his 30,000 feet of Le Mans footage and closed a deal with CBS/Cinema Center Films to finance the property. The film would begin in June, 1970, at Le Mans. There was much to do beforehand. . . .

Meanwhile, Steve found a new form of racing. Drinking beer with a group of cycle buddies after his return from Europe, he was "turned on" to a new type of off-road competition going on "down at ole Ascot."

Ascot Park, the storied oval raceway in central Los Angeles, had hosted the best in dirt track events for decades, but jeeps and dune buggies had now joined the sprint cars and midgets in what was being hailed as "the birth of a wild sport."

Off-road racing, until now, had generally been conducted over stretches of desert, beach or backcountry. No one had seriously considered staging it on a relatively small closed track until Ascot came into the picture. In many ways, however, the site was ideal for off-road racing, since the jeeps and buggies bumped over an intertwining series of dirt trails in the infield as well as a spectacular twenty-five-foot-high leap from a raised dirt mound, plus two other six-foot jumps during a single lap.

If a driver bobbled the jumps he could end up in a very wet duck pond, and there were also solid wooden barriers to avoid while drifting the tricky turns.

Listening to his friends' descriptions of the action at

Ascot fired Steve's interest. Accompanied by Jim Garner, with young son Chad in tow, Steve attended one of the night events at the speedway in August, 1969.

"It was as far out as anything I'd seen in racing," declared McQueen. "Cars flying through the air off the jumps, like ghosts under the stadium lights . . . and dirt flyin' and the crowd yelling. I went into the pits to talk to this guy I knew, a mechanic for Vic Hickey, and he had this Prinz, a little thing with maybe fourteen horsepower. He offered to let me take it around Ascot and I said fine. So I did. Then somebody else offered to let me try it in a buggy. So I gave it a go, had a real bash over the jumps and whoop-de-dos and it was nothing but great. When I gave the guy back his buggy I figured that ended it. But I was wrong."

The following afternoon Steve got a call. "Hey, I hear you're running at Ascot next week."

"Not me, man," said McQueen.

"Well, the papers got you pegged to race, and a lot of people are gonna be down there to see you go."

Steve pondered the situation. "I really didn't want to run there," he admitted. "I'd never really competed on a dirt track, and I knew I could get my melon bent way out of shape doin' those crazy jumps and all. But I thought, well, the people want to see me, so why not give it a shot and see how it shapes up."

He readied the same jeep he'd attempted to race at Riverside ("the one with the pop-up hood!") by changing the plugs, removing the air filter and putting on dirt tires.

"Turned out to be just fine for Ascot," he said. "We had four hundred horses goin' for us. Small block Chevy, with a three-speed hydro. Handled good in the dirt and was much faster than I thought it would be. I did well enough that first night to want to try again. In fact, I began competing there on a fairly regular basis that summer."

A typical Ascot go: The fender-bashing Tuesday night

main is in progress around the 58-mile dirt speedway with its seven turns and chassis-bending triple jumps. McQueen, doing 90 in the Chevy jeep, is fighting it out among the leaders. A cut-down buggy is violently center-punched by a jeepster and spins into the path of Steve's hard-charging machine. Panic braking doesn't help; McQueen is into the tangle with the mud-splattered machine ahead of him tumbling end for end, sparks shooting as steel meshes steel. The race is stopped. No one hurt, but several cars out. Steve is ready to go again. . . .

The event is restarted in a surge of high-torque engines, whose unmuffled thunder shakes the ground. Steve guns forward, makes the 25-foot jump, bounces, keeps charging, slides wide on a turn, is slapped by another jeep, spins and stalls. He starts again in next-to-last position, is furious with himself and turns on the steam, working up through the pack, banging into second behind the leader. Steve can't quite catch him by the flag, but he gets it all together and wins the trophy dash that same night. Top driving in anybody's league.

"He's a natural," said Vic Hickey after watching McQueen drive at Ascot. "He's got more savvy for this kind of thing than any other man I know."

Winning a trophy at Ascot is dangerous.

"When you get air-mailed over that main jump it's weird," McQueen declared. "On one stretch of roadway they've got six half-buried telephone poles for you to bounce over. They make your suspension stand up and yell 'ouch!'—but it's that main jump that spooks you."

In one Ascot event Steve chipped some teeth on the jump, as his front axle snapped. And he made no secret of his distaste for the lighting and fence arrangement.

"It's not well lit out there. You're going all out with almost two tons of machine under you, heading for that wooden fence at the end of the straight. If I'd gone into it I could have messed up a lot of people. They needed rails at the end of that straight. Besides which, to make things worse, you're usually out of brakes by the final laps. Brakes are always a problem at Ascot."

Though Steve's exploits on the dirt naturally disturbed Neile, his trophy-winning runs delighted their two children. Chad was much more impressed with his father as a racer than as an actor.

But acting was Steve's business, and that September he received another major honor: He flew to Washington to accept a trophy as "1969's Male Star of the Year" from the National Association of Theater Owners (NATO), representing 10,000 film houses in the United States. This award further reflected the runaway success of *Bullitt*. ("People are going back two and three times," Steve was told, "just to see that crazy race through the streets!")

McQueen's abiding concern with "problem kids" continued to manifest itself by his visits to the Boys Republic. He was accompanied on one such visit by a writer assigned to record the event for a major magazine. The writer was frankly suspicious of the actor's motives but soon came to accept them as genuine.

"He's good with these boys, very good," the writer admitted. "He shot pool with them for a couple of hours, told them he used to work in the laundry there. He jokes with them, listens to them and encourages them. They dig him. He's one of them, an ex-tough kid back on his turf, and he reaches them."

That same month McQueen became very upset over a news story headlined TWO BOYS SENTENCED TO ADULT PRISON. The account revealed that a Florida judge had sentenced Donald Douglas, fourteen, and Richard Copas, fifteen, to three years' confinement in an adult maximum-security prison. Their crime: "breaking and entering with intent to commit a misdemeanor."

Steve was shocked, angry. "Those kids don't belong in such a place," he said—and immediately phoned officials in Florida to offer his personal help. He was told there was nothing he could do, that only an appeal could change the sentence, and that the two boys must remain in the adult prison until an appeal could be heard. This could consume several months.

Steve refused to quit. He phoned Florida's State Health Secretary, James Bax, and declared that he was ready to make himself responsible for the youngsters, that he would get them into the Boys Republic, and that they *must* be removed from a place which could cripple them for life.

Bax said he didn't know if anything could be done, that they were already in Lake Butler Prison.

McQueen consulted his attorney, then talked to the authorities at Chino. He used his influence to reach the office of Claude Kirk, the governor of Florida, pleading for a chance to rescue the two boys.

A week passed, while Steve sweated. Then he received a call from James Bax. "Good news. The governor has broken precedent and has gone down to Lake Butler and removed the boys from prison. He's put them under his personal custody until they can be placed in our juvenile rehabilitation home in Marianna. Looks like we've won this time, Steve!"

McQueen let out a whoop of joy. He knew they'd be all right at Marianna. They'd have the same chance there that he had at Chino to make good in the adult world.

Steve had helped win a moral victory.

He was to seek another kind of victory before the year ended. There was still one great adventure ahead for him in 1969: His entry had been accepted for the Baja 1000.

10

FROM A BOOT AT BAJA TO A
POWERHOUSE PORSCHE

They called Baja the devil's playground, and with good reason. This long finger of desolate land stretching down along the Gulf of California is surely hell-spawned in its fire blast of sun and dust and raw rock. Attempting to drive the 800-plus miles from Ensenada to the tip at La Paz is impossibly difficult; to *race* over the same terrain is madness.

Yet, each year in November the Baja peninsula becomes the focal point for what must honestly be considered the world's most savage motor race.

They officially termed it a rally in 1967 for the first running of this event, but that tame label fooled no one; from flag to flag, Baja was a car-bashing, bone-busting, all-out race, won on guts, with the devil's luck to ride you home. In 1968 they simply called it the Baja 1000—and the race began to attract the best off-road drivers in the sport.

By 1969, when Steve McQueen entered the lists for the third annual event, the eyes of the racing world were on Baja. News helicopters were ready to follow the star drivers and documentary teams would film the action. Baja was now the "big one," the ultimate challenge for the best off-roaders.

The route down the rugged length of the peninsula included the start from Ensenada, eight checkpoints (at Camalu, El Rosario, Rancho Santa Inez, Punta Prieta, El Arco, San Ignacio, La Purisima, Villa Constitucion) and on to the finish at La Paz—a total of 832 miles, requiring more than twenty hours of day-night racing between souped-up trucks, bikes, buggies, jeeps and an odd assortment of "muscle" cars.

Steve's friendly rival, James Garner, was driving a Hickey-prepared Olds Cutlass, V-8 powered, in the production sedan class—which added spice to the race.

McQueen had gone down early to practice driving the route, first on a bike "to kind of feel it out" and then with his Chevy-powered Boot. He soon discovered just how rough Baja can get.

"I broke the Boot on every trial run I made down there," he declared. "Man, I must have slept in every barnyard on that peninsula. It's eight hundred miles of the last frontier."

For the race itself, Harold Daigh was "riding shotgun" next to Steve in the big red Boot. (Asked if he was nervous, Daigh snorted, "It could be worse. I could be playing Russian Roulette with all the chambers loaded.")

Beginning at 8 a.m., rolling between packed lines of eager spectators, the entrants (all 247 of them) roared off at staggered one-minute intervals from Ensenada on what was the fastest leg of the race (due to the fact that most of the road was paved into Camalu). Brute power counted most over this ninety-mile stretch, and McQueen's Boot

117

stormed along in fine style (paced by a camera-equipped Jet Ranger, flying directly above him all the way).

Tragedy struck early just south of the first checkpoint when a Ford Bronco rolled several times, killing its two drivers, while a dune buggy crash injured two other competitors (who were flown to a hospital).

The Boot kept charging, climbed into the mountains, sliding around hairpin turns flanked by five-hundred-foot dropoffs. The pavement ended, and the last miles into Camalu were rugged, as McQueen bumped over ruts and moon-crater potholes.

Clear of the first checkpoint, his route card stamped, Steve pushed forward, unaware of the deaths behind him. The Boot seemed capable of a win and he drove with confidence.

"In the fast sections," he said, "it was not unusual for us to get airborne for fifty to seventy feet over road dips. The Boot rides so smooth you can overdo things. Even in bad, choppy sections it'll do sixty or so, and if you slam into a big rock at that speed you can crack an axle or worse."

Machines were dropping out of the race with slashed tires, blown transmissions, cracked blocks, broken steering arms, rock-punctured radiators . . . as Baja exacted its fierce toll. Only 97 entrants would limp in to the finish at La Paz; 150 would not.

The road grew progressively rougher into El Rosario, the second checkpoint. Steve gunned the Boot down the narrow canyon trail into this town, which marked the terminus of telephone communication. Beyond El Rosario, known as "the last outpost," the race entered the wilds of central Baja. The guidebooks advised motorists to proceed "with extreme caution."

McQueen was not driving by the book; extreme caution would cost him the race. Card stamped, the Boot thundered away for Rancho Santa Inez, eighty-six miles farther down the rock-ribbed peninsula. The route was nightmarish—a hellish mixture of sage, huge boulders (which racing men call "rim crackers"), boglike silt and looming cardon cactus. With a roar that shook the dried boogum blossoms, McQueen blasted through this impassable wilderness, goggles misted with dust, his mouth caked with gritty sand. He was still moving very swiftly, holding a solid overall position among the fastest machines. He could still win.

The miles spun past. Steve's radiator began to smoke. No water. "We're dry!" yelled Daigh.

Steve nodded, but kept rolling.

They spotted another car, a Ford Bronco. An observation vehicle, not a competitor.

"We need water," yelled McQueen. "Got some to spare?"

"Sure do."

They hastily filled the steaming radiator.

"You see Garner in the Olds?" asked McQueen.

"Yeah," said the Bronco driver. "He went by here more than an hour ago."

"Thanks!"

The Boot fish-tailed away, wheels biting gravel. Steve wanted to nail Garner; he figured his Boot should best the Olds to La Paz. Unless he got unlucky.

He did. Just before the third checkpoint the Boot began to slow down. There was an ominous rasping sound from the automatic transmission.

"We've had it," Steve groaned, stripping off his dust-clogged goggles and easing himself from the cockpit.

A small teflon gear had failed in the transmission, which put the car out for good. Just 238 miles into the race, Steve parked the crippled Boot at Rancho Santa Inez and took a private jet back to Los Angeles.

Jim Garner went on to notch a well-driven second in class, and the overall winner (in 20 hours, 48 minutes) was a Ford Bronco. Reversing the Mint 7-11 results, the first bike to finish was fifth as the four-wheelers had their revenge.

The last engine was stilled. Silence settled like a slow drift of smoke over the timeless land. Baja, 1969, was part of racing history.

For Steve McQueen, it was a challenge accepted, a job done. He would be coming back one day to fight this land again. And perhaps, in a luckier year, he would conquer it.

By February, 1970 Steve was again in Hollywood headlines, having been voted "Golden Globe World Film Favorite" in a poll conducted in forty-one countries by Reuters. Due to this unquestioned global popularity his film price had risen to a cool million per picture, and scripts were flooding in to him.

But Steve had his own ideas on what films he wanted to make. He talked of a Solar-owned property called *Yucatan*, to be filmed in the wilds of Mexico.

"There's a fortune down there waiting in Yucatan," he said, discussing the background of the story. "Seems that way back about nine hundred years ago the Indians used to deck out young Mayan girls—literally cover them with jewels, the weight of which would carry these sacrificial maidens to the bottom of sacred wells. The legend is that all those jewels are still there in those hidden wells. Our story would center on a guy who takes his cycle into the Mexican wilds on a personal treasure hunt. An adventure film, with deep-sea diving and lots of bike action. We're still in the planning stage with this one. But when we get it right we'll make it and naturally I'll play the guy on the cycle."

Steve's film on Le Mans would come first, and he knew that in order to prepare himself for this high-speed assignment he would have to "sharpen up in a good piece of machinery." Meaning he needed a truly competitive car to drive.

The machine he chose was a power-laden Porsche 908,

the model which had come within a hair of winning Le Mans in 1969, when Steve was a spectator in France. He'd been mightily impressed with the 908's race potential and (through CBS) had arranged to purchase this ex-factory machine for his Solar stable.

"Le Mans is a very fast race," Steve explained. "I needed to familiarize myself with a car like the 908 in order to drive Le Mans with any kind of authentic feel for the course. In most Hollywood racing movies the star is doubled. He never really drives. I didn't want any doubles for me at Le Mans. If I couldn't cut it there then I figured there was no point in making the film. That was my view, and CBS went along with me."

Realizing that the 908 would require expert preparation and maintenance, Steve contacted ex-Grand Prix star Richie Ginther. One of motor racing's outstanding talents, Ginther had retired from competition driving in 1967 but was still involved in the sport.

"Ole Rich is a brave man, a very daring fellow," Steve said. "And he knows Porsches. Raced them for years. With him setting up the 908 I knew I'd get the full power potential out of the car. The rest was up to me."

They took the Porsche to Willow Springs to sort it out. Steve throttled the road-hugging white racer onto the circuit and found more power under his foot than he could handle. The car spun and stalled. McQueen tried again. A hot run, then another spinout. He was learning, deliberately pushing the 908 hard to find its limits.

Tuning. Adjusting. Another run. Smoother now. And fast. Very, very fast. By the end of that initial practice session at Willow, McQueen and Ginther knew they had "a going beast."

"We decided, just for the fun of it, to enter a club event," said Steve. "At that point I really didn't consider running the car at Sebring, I just wanted to see what I could do with it at Holtville."

The course record at Holtville had been set at 1:15 by hotshoe Scooter Patrick in a swift Alfa T-33 in 1969. When Steve rolled onto the California circuit in his white Porsche for the official practice session in February, 1970, he was there to learn the course, not set records. But the car responded so well Steve couldn't resist a shot at Patrick's mark. He uncorked the 908 in a blistering run that chopped two full seconds off the Alfa record.

There was no stopping him. In the main event, as the other cars fell back, Steve lapped the entire field (except for second-place runner Herb Caplan, who finished 58 seconds behind him).

Steve's decisive victory in this Sports Car Club of America event at Holtville encouraged him to have a go at the upcoming Riverside SCCA road races.

Riverside was a much tougher driving assignment, but McQueen looked forward to competing in the 908 Porsche. He'd once borrowed a Lola T-70 to learn the circuit and, until now, the Lola was the hottest car he'd run there.

"Winning at Riverside takes a lot of horsepower for that mile-long back straight," Steve said, then described an average lap over the course. "Start-finish is on a short straight. Turn one is an uphill left-hander and quite tricky because you go in blind, all the way over to the right, then cut to the left-hand side and come out sliding. Then you throw the car into opposite lock for a downhill right-hander, which is turn two. Then you're into the Esses, maximum speed around 125. Three is left, four is right and five is left again. Then you climb uphill into turn six, braking to 65. It's a right-hander with a tightening radius and a guardrail that's just waiting for you to bobble. Seven is a downhill left-hander, eight a modest right-hander—and then you set your car for that long straight. I did 157 there my first time out in the Lola, but you can go as high as your engine and your nerve will take you. At the end of the straight, as you come to the shutoff markers for turn nine, you get all the way left and start your hard-braking and downshifting. This last turn is deceptive, a long right-hander that just keeps tightening on you. It's quite easy to run out of road on nine, which you must not do. Halfway through, you give your car a little jog to set it up for the pit straight and the run to the finish."

What McQueen didn't talk about was the fact that the great Ken Miles had died on turn nine, as had other drivers, and that Riverside, from its first race, has been a deadly, unforgiving circuit. A severe spin almost anywhere on the course could have fatal results.

When Steve raced the 908 at Riverside Neile was there as a nervous spectator; she watched her talented husband set fast time on Saturday and win a minor event that afternoon. Steve was cool, confident, pleased with the car—but Neile couldn't relax. She sensed that serious trouble waited for Steve in Sunday's main. And she was right.

"On Sunday by the seventh lap I was leading the race," McQueen related. "We were running Le Mans gears because of the long straight, which gave us 160 in fourth. On the previous lap I'd been dicing a Lola. He was right on my tail down the back straight, but he bobbled and spun directly behind me going into nine. So I was in good shape. I'd put a little air between me and the second-place runner, giving me a comfortable edge toward a win. Then, on this seventh lap, I'd cleared nine and had shifted from third into fourth again on the pit straight, lining up for turn one, which was blind and fairly swift.

"I was committed to my line into the turn at about 150 when—blam!—the whole gearbox exploded under me! Neile, who witnessed the thing, said she could see black pieces of metal blown high into the air. The fourth gear had blown right off the counter shaft and knocked a big hole in the crankcase, which automatically socked me into neutral.

I began to wipe across the track, from one side to the other, using up all the road. It was real nip-and-tuck there for a while and I didn't know if I'd come out in one piece or not. Scared hell out of me!"

Steve nosed the smoking Porsche to a final stop by the road edge and pulled himself out of the car. "What we need," he said to his gray-faced pit crew as he stripped off helmet and goggles, "is a new gearbox."

They got one for Phoenix. Installing a new box flown in from Germany, Richie had the 908 ready for this Arizona race on the first day of March: the Phoenix Winter Sprint, a 17-lap feature event around the 10-turn, 2.7-mile circuit. In this charity run, with the proceeds going to the Arizona Boys Ranch, McQueen was again in top form.

The near-crash at Riverside had not shaken him. He set a new lap record of 1:41:9 at Phoenix and handily defeated this 16-car field (despite a brisk bid from Eric Hauser's Lola).

This victory put him into the SCCA's top slot for Class A, but he wasn't able to follow up his points lead due to other factors. Factors such as Lake Elsinore on a cycle and Sebring in the 908, both that same month. (He also filed his entry for the Mint 400, intending to run a special Chevy truck there as a direct follow-up to Sebring.)

"When I broke my foot at Elsinore unloading over the bars," said Steve, "that messed me up for the Mint. I got through the Florida 12-Hours okay, with Pete and me lucky enough to notch our class win and overall second, but the doc nixed my running the Mint after Sebring. So I stayed home and nursed my foot while Bud Ekins drove one of our Solar entries."

Ekins earned a second in class, despite rolling the Solar machine early in the race when the side of a silt hill gave way under his wheels.

"We're getting a real goer ready for the next Mint," declared Steve. "Scaled-down, shortened, four-wheel-drive

Blazer with a neat 427 Chevy engine in a fiber glass body. I want to see what I can do with *that* one!"

McQueen kept planning, preparing himself and his machinery for future races. But his immediate plans centered around a small farming village in France.

Le Mans.

11

DANGER AT LE MANS

Americans fly at Kitty Hawk!

Wright Brothers defy gravity in fantastic new air machine!

The news stunned Europe. Invitations were sent out: Would the daring flyers come to France and demonstrate their incredible airplane?

Wilbur Wright accepted. He arrived in Europe and set out to locate a suitable section of land from which to launch his aircraft. A site was finally selected in the farming country of midwestern France 120 miles from Paris, where the French Grand Prix of 1906 had been held. And it was here, on August 8, 1908, that the first air exhibition in Europe took place.

At Le Mans.

In 1921 another American gained fame at Le Mans with a piece of U.S. machinery when driver Jimmy Murphy won the Grand Prix of France in a boat-tailed Dusenberg.

Two years later a racketing field of improbable vehicles smoked away down the straight for the first Le Mans 24-Hours—and the greatest endurance race in motoring history was born. Over the years 1923 through 1969 a total of thirty-seven round-the-clock events were run at Le Mans, won by an impressive list of marques: The powerful red Ferraris carried off nine victories; Jaguar and Bentley notched five each; Alfa Romeo won four times; and American Fords took the checker in 1966, 1967, 1968 and 1969. (Along-the-way race winners included such lost-and-forgotten marques as Chenard-Walcker, Lorraine-Dietrich, Lagonda, Talbot, Delahaye and several more.)

A Porsche had never won the overall prize at Le Mans, but Ford had barely edged out the German cars in 1969. A win was long overdue, and 1970 was the year of the Porsche. The fantastic new 12-cylinder, 600-hp 917's were odds-on favorites to win the 24-Hours, and Steve McQueen was well aware of their potential.

He was finally ready to move on his Le Mans racing film, and he chose a $70,000 factory 917 Porsche as his mount for the venture. The world's fastest sports car, this machine was capable of hitting 240 and better down the Mulsanne straight at Le Mans. In sheer horsepower it matched the fabled old Auto Unions of Hitler's Germany, yet was lighter than a Volkswagen! CBS/Cinema Center Films agreed to let Steve have his very potent Porsche, providing he did *not* race it in the official 24-Hours as he'd planned.

"That was a blow," he confessed. "We'd made arrangements with the 1969 world Champion, Jackie Stewart, to co-drive the 917 with me. We were going to have cameras set up in our pit to film all the driver-fuel stops. Then, after the race, we'd integrate all this footage into our picture. But my driving at Sebring with a broken foot had scared off the CBS people, and Le Mans was out.

They had eight million of their dollars riding on me, so I agreed to pull our entry. Told Jackie no go. But it hurt, it really hurt. The thing is, with a car like the 917 we *could* have won!"

Perhaps CBS had been influenced by Mario Andretti's printed statement to the effect that "Le Mans is the most dangerous race in the world." One of its special hazards involves the fact that smaller cars, with a top of 100-plus mph, must be passed at night, often in fog and rain, by the big monsters doing well over 200. In 1955 Le Mans became the site of motor racing's greatest tragedy, as a Mercedes struck a smaller Healey and plowed into a crowd of spectators along the pit straight, killing eighty-three of them as well as the Mercedes driver, Pierre Levegh.

Le Mans has claimed the lives of many competitors. The first driver fatality occurred during the third running of the 24-Hours in 1925, and during subsequent years (into 1969) at least a dozen others have crashed to their deaths a Le Mans. Practice in 1969 took the life of popular Lucian Bianchi, and the race itself claimed John Woolfe (who died in the fiery crash of a 917 Porsche practically identical to McQueen's model).

Thus, in view of the alarming statistics, CBS had a valid reason for keeping Steve out of the 1970 event. But the fact that he was forbidden to enter the race did not affect his plans to field his smaller 908 Porsche there as a camera car, with Herbert Linge of West Germany and Jonathan Williams of England as co-drivers. Getting an okay was difficult: Le Mans officials were, at first, solidly against allowing a camera-equipped car into the race. (In practice, another 908 tangled with a Matra and was torn in half.) The officials were afraid that the McQueen-entered 908, with its three cameras, might create a particular road hazard, but Steve overcame these objections by proving that the cameras had been mounted to form an integral part of the chassis (one was fitted under a bubble in the hood) and that there was no chance that loose parts would fall onto the track.

"We *had* to have actual race footage," he explained. "Without it, we'd have no vital point-of-view shots. At the going rate for extras, which was twelve dollars per head per day, trying to duplicate the vast crowd at Le Mans was impossible. You don't hire half a million extras! We planned to restage the pit action, using maybe fifteen hundred extras, but we needed that in-race footage to catch the main mass of people along the length of the circuit."

Steve won his argument. The Solar entry was allowed to compete, and McQueen's pit prepared to supply cans of film as well as the usual gas, oil and tires for the 908.

Steve was not satisfied with the condition of the circuit. Many parts of it he found dark and drab, unsuitable for his color cameras. Therefore, with the delighted permission of the officials, he gave his crew the job of brightening Le Mans. Among other improvements, Solar workers completely repainted the pits and added new circuit lights at key corners such as Tertre Rouge and Maison Blanche.

The 1970 Le Mans 24-Hours was a bitterly contested affair, with no less than 11 Ferrari 512's battling 7 Porsche 917's for the big win. Alfas, Matras and several other marques were also in the lists, but the main conflict raged between the factory-backed Italian and German machines and men: Ferrari *vs.* Porsche.

The long-tailed 917 of Vic Elford was clocked at 225 down the Mulsanne straight, and the 512's were just as fast. Had McQueen and Stewart fielded the Solar 917 they would no doubt have found themselves locked into a blood duel for the lead position. As it was, the Solar 908 never had a chance for a top slot; the drivers were content to trail the faster cars and keep their machine running until the end.

Le Mans lived up to its dangerous reputation: Four of the 512 Ferraris were involved in a metal-bending pile-up past the tricky White House section of the 8.4-mile circuit, and Jackie Ickx (the 1969 winner), running second in the rain, attempted to squeeze his 512 Ferrari into a one-lane S-turn ahead of a 917. He didn't make it and was forced to slam on the brakes; the rear wheels locked and the red Ferrari spun into a road bank, killing a turn marshal.

Le Mans, 1970, was won by Hans Herrmann and Richard Attwood in a 917, marking the first-ever Porsche victory in this event. Only 17 of the 51 entries lasted the full twenty-four hours. The Solar 908 finished second in class and eighth overall, despite its many stops for film reloads. Its three cameras (plus sixteen others spaced around the circuit) gave McQueen over 90,000 feet of racing footage.

Normally, Le Mans is open to traffic during the rest of the year (since it incorporates several miles of public road), but McQueen's company paid the officials a $30,000 fee to rent the circuit for use in their film. Once this was cleared, Solar Village was built near the paddock area in order to house the 150-man production crew. The village sprawled over 100,000 square feet, and miles of electrical wiring and water pipes were laid through the French countryside. A restaurant was constructed, designed to feed up to 300 people per meal. Additionally, many professional drivers were hired to double for actors during on-track staged racing sequences.

"We got some real talent," said McQueen. "Mike Parkes was our racing consultant, and he drove for us. So did Jackie Ickx, Jo Siffert, Masten Gregory, Vic Elford, Dick Attwood, Jonathan Williams, David Piper, Derek Bell and many more."

Solar also lined up what amounted to a million-dollar racing stable for the picture, buying or leasing some two dozen top cars. When Enzo Ferrari was approached regarding use of some 512's from his factory he demanded to see the script. "Who wins?" he asked. "Ferrari or Porsche?"

He was told a Porsche wins in the film, and he promptly refused to allow use of his cars. Solar nevertheless found some private owners who agreed to supply 512's, and McQueen arranged to have Ferrari body shells built over two Corvette-powered Lolas for use in crash segments.

Among the cars acquired for use in *Le Mans* were four 917 Porsches, two 908's, some production 911's and a scattering of Lolas, Alfas and Matras, along with five Ferraris. Each had spare engines, sets of wet and dry tires and extra wheels. (A plane stood by during the shooting, used to pick up any needed parts at Stuttgart or Modena.) McQueen had imported the Indy expert Haig Alltounian as chief mechanic to supervise the Solar stable of crack machinery.

Camera car for *Le Mans* was a modified GT-40 Ford (the same machine which had won several European races). Powered with a V-8 4.7-liter engine, and handled by stunt driver Rob Slotemaker, the GT was capable of pacing any car on the track. Solar had purchased it from Ford, had sliced off its top, converting it to an open-cockpit model.

"The steel monocoque chassis was ideally constructed when it came to the cutting and welding necessary to lay in our cameras," said McQueen. "Much of this work was done in England before the start of our film."

With the welding and cutting completed, the Ford was handed over to Hollywood's Gaylin Schultz, who mounted the complex, expensive cameras on the GT-40. A stationary 35-mm Arriflex faced rearward in the center of the chassis behind the driver; a second camera unit was fitted into an aluminum, foam-lined bubble seat beside the driver, in which operator Alex Barbey handled the swivel-mounted 35-mm Mitchell, adapted for Panovision lenses.

(There were also special technical adaptations which allowed Barbey to pan and tilt as desired in order to follow a fast-moving 917 Porsche or 512 Ferrari through full 180-degree approach-and-pass sequences.)

Driving the Ford was extremely tricky, since it had to move alongside racing machines at full chat on narrow sections of road, taking an outside line through corners meant for a single car. Cool Rob Slotemaker was precisely the man for such hazardous work, since he had gained fame operating a series of highly successful "skid schools" in Germany, Switzerland and Holland. ("We teach student drivers how to put their cars safely into 180-degree or 360-degree skids for sport or for road defense.")

Among the many specialists hired for *Le Mans* was a "bug man." His job was to squash bugs realistically against windscreens to duplicate the effect of actual Le Mans driving conditions. Other specialists included "circuit dressers." These men would "dress" the entire circuit each morning of shooting with the proper flags, banners, etc.—then "undress" it each night.

A carnival atmosphere is very much a part of Le Mans, and McQueen was forced to rent all of the rides and booths which ordinarily crowd the infield each year. Here he ran his own night carnival for certain dramatic scenes in the film, re-creating the "giant amusement park" aura of life behind the grandstands.

Many changes had been made in Le Mans history; the original circuit was totally destroyed in the 1940's, with the bomb-rutted roadways rebuilt in the postwar years. After the 1955 tragedy the front straight was widened. Later a chicane was added to slow the cars coming onto the front straight, and a steel guardrail had recently been built around the entire circuit. Le Mans is a very swift race, mainly due to its long, 3.2-mile straight known as Mulsanne on which McQueen's 917 attained speeds in excess of 225. Getting used to driving such a monster took some doing for Steve; he'd never been in as fast a car.

"The 917 is unlike other racing machines I've driven," he said, "in that it makes its move, then delivers the impulse to you *afterward*. In most cars you feel what's going to happen before it happens and can adjust. The 917 is always a bit ahead of you in making up its mind about things. You must be extremely alert and stay on top of it."

McQueen refused to allow any fake process shots for *Le Mans*. His intention was to show the event as it is really run, which meant driving at full-race speeds in front of the cameras.

John Sturges, the director who'd been selected for *Le Mans* after the fiasco on *Day of the Champion*, had strong ideas: "We want to capture the mood of this event as well as the dangers—get the whole thing on film from the crowds coming in, the cars being unloaded, the tension building toward the start. . . . We want to show the race by day and on into the rainy night. Le Mans is a unique event because at five in the morning, when most of the crowd is sleeping in tents and trailers around the course, here are these drivers, out there on the ragged edge, cutting laps in the fog, hitting over 200 on Mulsanne. . . . We want to show all that, capture it all."

No one seemed to know, well into the shooting, just what the picture concerned in terms of a dramatic personal story. Several writers had drafted versions of the screenplay, but by June, 1970, when the Solar unit began filming, Sturges and McQueen were still not settled on a shooting script. At $40,000 a day, the production was at sea on a story.

"Basically," said Steve, "we wanted the film to reflect the conflict of a gladiator in the arena. We wanted to avoid all the hoary old racing clichés done in so many other pictures. I had this idea about doing it with an absolute minimum of dialogue, with the *race* as the focal point. No sex or sensationalism. Racing is a beautiful sport. I'm very serious about doing it justice. Sure, we'll have some crashes in the film because cars *do* crash at Le Mans. But this one will be totally honest, with no compromises. I would never shortchange a sport that's meant so much to me in my life."

When Neile arrived in France with the children Steve rented a massive, thirty-room villa for them in the country near the village of Le Mans. Neile found much beauty in the placid cattle and wheat-farming community but did not enjoy the sight of her husband roaring around the circuit at killing speeds. She took the children on a European tour "to get them away, for a while at least, from racers and racing."

McQueen kept pushing for a final storyline, and with the help of auto writer Ken Purdy (called in to "polish" Harry Kleiner's basic screenplay) he finally got one: He would play an ice-hard pro named Michael Delaney who had crashed the previous year at Le Mans and who was trying for a comeback win in a Gulf Porsche 917. He faced his great rival, Erich Stahler, who was driving a 512 Ferrari. Delaney's crash had claimed the life of another driver, Belgetti, and this man's widow, Lisa, had returned to Le Mans, drawn to Delaney, yet still bitter over her husband's death. During the race Delaney is balked by a slower car and once again crashes. But the Porsche team manager puts him into another 917 and he engages Stahler in a fierce duel in the final stages of the event. Too far back to claim outright victory, he nevertheless edges out Stahler, finishes second—and wins the girl.

In one key scene, Lisa asks Delaney why men race, and he tells her that racing is a way of life for the men who do it well. Anything between is "just waiting." To race well, to do a dangerous thing perfectly, this is the racer's goal. Nothing else really matters. She doesn't fully understand, but she accepts—and a bond is formed between them.

One sequence called for Delaney to pass Stahler's 512

Ferrari inside a turn at speed on a wet track. Any pro in the company could easily have doubled for McQueen in this sequence (since moviegoers would not be able to tell one driver from another in face mask and helmet), but Steve would not hear of a switch. He meant to do *all* of his own driving, including the dangerous stunts, and what moviegoers could or could not see did not matter to him. Not in this regard.

The GT-40 rumbled into position, with Barbey ready at the camera. The production spray trucks had finished watering down the section of track from Mulsanne corner to the Arnage turn, and the driver of the 512 Ferrari gave thumbs-up to a helmeted and waiting McQueen, now strapped and harnessed into the 917.

Sturges gave the roll 'em signal, and the big Porsche exploded into mechanical life. Steve eased the long blue machine onto the circuit, taking it rapidly up through the gears, paced by the Ferrari and the GT Ford.

The sequence was attempted: At speed, with the camera grinding, McQueen made his pass, laying the 917 hard into a sweeping 150-mph right-hand bend. But the action didn't come off to his liking, so they did it again. This time Steve seemed pleased.

"Yeah, we were on the edge out there," he told a reporter. "It's bloody dangerous, passing at speed on a wet track that way. No room for error. I was running with my left front tire on the white line, only about a foot and a half from the iron guardrail. I figured if I lost it I'd try and slap the rail and ride it along rather than bounce back on the road and take a chance on getting center-punched by the GT."

At one point in the filming Steve's life was on the line. Breasting a slight rise on Mulsanne in the 917, he was set to pass a car ahead at 200 mph with the camera GT riding at full chat next to him, recording the action. The three cars boomed down the long straight, cleared the rise—and faced potential disaster. In the middle of the straight, motoring serenely toward them, was a massive Solar service truck. The driver had been told that the day's shooting was over, and the last thing he expected to meet on Mulsanne was this trio of fast-charging race cars.

It was close. The truck pulled over, scraping the rail, while the racers ripped past, sliding and fish-tailing, their drivers fighting for control. Nobody crashed. Nobody hurt. Close.

Unfortunately, in two other instances the results were much more serious. Derek Bell was throttling one of the $65,000 Ferraris down Mulsanne at over 200 when smoke began pouring from the car; the electrical system had malfunctioned and the Ferrari was aflame. Before Bell could get the car stopped the gas tank exploded, bathing him in flame. A Le Mans ruling requires that all drivers wear flameproof clothing capable of withstanding the temperature of burning gasoline for 15 seconds. This ruling saved Bell's life; he was pulled from the car, but his face and hands were severely burned. The Ferrari was a fire-gutted writeoff.

On another afternoon of shooting, over a different section of the circuit, David Piper lost one of the potent 917's and slammed the rail, spun wildly, slamming into the rail again 325 feet farther down the track. Breaking into pieces, the Porsche threw its wheels 150 yards into a lettuce patch. Piper was rushed to the hospital with a triple compound fracture of the right leg. In London, doctors worked desperately to save the leg but were eventually forced to amputate below the knee.

McQueen duplicated this accident in the film (although, as Delaney he survived the crash unhurt). The script called for Delaney to come up too fast on a smaller car, brake and lose control, spin and crash, slamming the 917 to pieces against the guardrails on either side of the track. This staged smashup and another just preceding it surpassed anything ever done on film and gives the moviegoer the gut-sensation of having crashed a racing machine at speed.

"We actually took a remote-controlled car," said McQueen, "and engineered a precise mistake like one that would cause a racing driver to lose control. We covered the crash with fourteen cameras, three of them in slow motion, the other eleven from different angles. Then we cut this together so you could actually see what a man goes through in the crash. You see him make his mistake; you see the car go out of control and crash—all in normal fast motion. As the crushed, smoking machine comes to rest, the camera, you, looks in through the shattered windshield at the driver's eyes. The camera seems to enter his head, his thoughts, and the entire crash is unreeled in slow motion, telling you what he sees and feels as he relives the accident. It's shocking, scalp-lifting, unlike anything ever done on a screen."

In these carefully staged accidents several cars were demolished, to a total cost of $300,000. Which worried CBS officials back on the West Coast. (McQueen had missed a shift and blown the engine on his 917, which also added to the rising production costs.)

Several top CBS executives flew to Le Mans for emergency talks. A two-week shutdown was called. Rumors rippled through Solar Village: would they cancel the picture? Was *Le Mans* to go the way of *Day of the Champion*?

Swedish TV actress Louise Edlind had been signed for one of the two main female leads (as the wife of a driver on the verge of quitting the profession) and as the widow of the driver killed in the Delaney crash Solar had signed Elga Anderson. Would they be dismissed along with the three dozen drivers and other actors?

No, Steve assured his crew, the film would be

137

completed. The script needed more work, but CBS had agreed to continue financing. The shutdown was temporary.

For John Sturges it was permanent: He declared that working with an uncompleted screenplay was not to his liking and while Neile and Steve were in Morocco he packed his bags and returned to the States. Director Lee Katzin, whose reputation was gained in television, was brought in to replace Sutrges when shooting resumed.

"Steve had a very strong idea of how he wanted this film handled," declared Katzin. "He wanted to do something very close to a pure documentary, holding story and dialogue to a minimum and letting the race itself dominate. John Sturges, on the other hand, wanted to build characters and story over the racing, allowing the *people* to dominate. Me, I just wanted to make a good movie!"

In the final version of the script the rivalry was intensified between Stahler (portrayed by actor Siegfried Rauch) and Delaney, although their dialogue was held to a few muted lines. Their fierce duel on the track in the final laps resulted in some of the screen's most exciting race footage.

One of the men hired to drive the cars in *Le Mans* was motorcycle champion Mike Hailwood, and McQueen did not fail to take advantage of this fact. He rode against Hailwood many times that summer, using the smaller Bugatti Circuit in the area and alternating on three bikes: his Triumph Bonneville, a Norton Commando and his Husky 400. Thus, Steve was "keeping sharp" on two wheels as well as four.

Even his young son, Chad, got into the action. Piloting a miniature Ferrari on a special boys' circuit, the nine-year-old McQueen did his father proud by entering a race they called *Quatre Jours Du Mans* and defeating fifteen other competitors.

The speed bug was indeed active at Le Mans, and

several members of the production crew discovered the joys and dangers of fast motoring. So many privately owned cars were smashed up in between-takes dicing that a new group was formed described by a member as "the Le Mans Daredevil Driving and Beer Drinking Society —membership in which is earned by wrecking your car on the circuit."

Le Mans took five months to film (from June into November) and every sequence was shot directly on the course or in the immediate area.

"We brought 450,000 feet of film back to the States to edit," said Katzin. "It took six months of looping, dubbing, splicing and cutting to get a final work print. We had to match fifty-five sound tracks, including one for each racing car, plus laying in the music."

No studio faking had been allowed, and when the picture was released in the summer of 1971, it was impossible for moviegoers to tell what was real and what wasn't. Footage from the actual Le Mans race had been so well integrated with staged footage that the effect was seamless and totally authentic. The 4 p.m. Saturday to 4 p.m. Sunday marathon had been brilliantly rendered.

When newsmen asked Steve if this one had been rough, the star chuckled. "Rough? It was a bloodbath—the most dangerous thing I've ever done. I'm lucky I'm still alive. But we were honest. We did it *right*, and that's what matters."

For the actor who races and the racer who acts, another important goal had been reached, another dream realized.

And, as he had promised, there were no compromises.

12

McQUEEN, TODAY AND TOMORROW

Despite his fascination and involvement with fast cars, Steve McQueen continues to make it plain that bikes are his first love. He returned from the Le Mans location to enter a cycle race at Indian Dunes, California, where he took home a trophy for third. He also financed a feature-length documentary on cycle competition, *On Any Sunday*, which included footage of his racing at Elsinore. When he speaks of the two-wheelers his emotional commitment is obvious.

"I've never been in a restaurant where I didn't perk an ear when a good cycle goes by. A Husqvarna 405 at about 12,000 rpm—that's music! In bike racing, I specialize. I don't do any flat track stuff, or TT's, that's not for me. No speedway stuff. I do rough-country riding, the long-distance kind of thing. I love the ground, the earth; I don't love asphalt. With a cycle, you're dealing with natural terrain, you learn to read the earth. . . . I like being out in the desert on a set of wheels. You're really *alive* out there. If I see a rabbit tear off I can chase after him. If I see some Indian petroglyphs on the rocks I can stop there, study them. . . . I just sit out there, alone, maybe for an hour or so, looking, feeling . . . with a 360-degree view of the world. Nobody to bother me."

Near his desert home, beyond Palm Springs, there's a sand wash that leads all the way into Indio. "I can drop right down into that wash and run for forty miles, all out, and maybe follow a plume of dust to find out who's behind it. Turns out to be another guy ridin' his bike same as I'm ridin' mine. We sit and rap for a while, like in the old barnstorming days when two strangers could land their crates in a Kansas field and talk about flying."

Steve sees his future in his children, who are now on the verge of entering their teen years. His daughter has already distinguished herself by winning a citizenship award, in addition to earning the second-highest marks at her school. Steve's son has his father's natural bent for machinery, and both youngsters are sports-minded. They enjoy campouts and fishing and sleeping under a clear sky. "I want my kids to mature in honest affection and understanding, without any of the hate that nearly consumed me as a boy," said Steve. "I'm not trying to run their lives for them, but I *am* going to try to show them the right way. They must learn that we all have a choice as to who and what we finally become. I want them to make the right decisions."

He's anti-drugs, feeling that "life itself is a trip, and all you need is some honest enthusiasm for what you do." He feels proud of the fact that he was born under the sign of Aries, the Ram. Those born under this sign share aggressive instincts and physical courage; they are ambitious, energetic, and tough.

His toughness has been demonstrated in every film he's made, including *Junior Bonner*, completed in Prescott, Arizona, in August, 1971. Steve played a has-been rodeo champ in this dusty, gut-busting epic, in which he emerged saddle-sore and fed up with bucking broncs. ("I prefer my horses under the hood.")

However, he got some personal satisfaction out of the trip to Arizona since he was able to aid some distressed Yavapai Indians near the film's location. Steve arranged two public screenings of *On Any Sunday*, donating all ticket money to the tribe.

Steve appreciates beauty in women, but he's still a one-woman man. The McQueen marriage, by Hollywood standards, is a miracle. It has endured, despite heated words and arguments, while the marriages of those around him have failed. For one thing, Steve appreciates Neile's offbeat personality. "Do you know what she gave me for Christmas last year?" he grinned. "She gave me this World War II half-track, a ten-ton Army job with iron treads and armor plating and with a 200-hp White under the bonnet. Now how about *that* for a Christmas present!"

Dissolve.

Fade in: a stretch of wide, lonely California desert in the backcountry near Indio. The sun is well up in a clear and cloudless sky. A soft wind stirs the puckerbushes, and, far off, but increasing in volume, is the faint insect buzz of a Husqvarna Motocross at speed. A rider is approaching, slamming his machine hard over the ridged sand, sliding around rocks and cactus, wheeling closer.

The sound of the Husky is now a throbbing roar as a helmeted McQueen throttles past, tanned and shirtless, jumping a sand ditch, smiling at nothing and nobody.

Voice over (McQueen): "Billy Graham once asked me what my religion was and I told him, 'It's the desert, the grass, the sun in the sky, my wife and kids—and my wheels.' "

The image of the cycle rider ripples and diminishes along the heat-hazed horizon.

Fade out.

ACKNOWLEDGMENTS

Since nonfiction is by nature a collaborative art I have drawn upon a wide variety of sources in writing this book. Therefore, to those I have quoted, questioned, consulted, I tender grateful acknowledgment.

My thanks to the following individuals: Mario Andretti, Jane Ardmore, Trevor Armbrister, Dean Batchelor, Knox Burger, Henry P. Burn, John Cooper, Frank Conroy, James T. Crow, Robert Daley, Faye Dunaway, Bud and Dave Ekins, Vincent Fennelly, Richie Ginther, Frank Graves, Henry Gris, Ernest Havemann, John Huetter, Robert Johnson, Arthur Knight, Neile McQueen, Edwin Miller, Charles Miron, Stirling Moss, Jay Richards, Betty Rollin, Ken Rudeen, Bill Sanders, Joe Scalzo, Edouard Seidler, John Skow, John Sturges, Tedd Thomey, Vincent Tubbs, Carol Veazie, Robert Wise.

My thanks, also, to the following organizations and libraries: the Academy library, the American Motorcycle Association, the Los Angeles *Times*, the Sports Car Club of America.

And, most particularly, my thanks to Steve McQueen.